DATE DUE			
OCT 2 5 1993			

THE FUTURE OF WOMEN

Rona M. Fields
Senior Partner & Director of Associates
in Community Psychology

GENERAL HALL, INC.
Publishers
23–45 Corporal Kennedy Street
Bayside, New York 11360

THE FUTURE OF WOMEN

GENERAL HALL, INC.

23-45 Corporal Kennedy Street
Bayside, New York 11360

Publisher: Ravi Mehra
Editor: Eileen Ostermann
Composition: *Graphics Division,* General Hall, Inc.

LIBRARY OF CONGRESS CATALOG CARD NUMBER: **84-081427**

ISBN: 0-930390-59-8 [paper]
0-930390-60-1 [cloth]

Manufactured in the United States of America

ABOUT THE AUTHOR

Rona M. Fields, Ph.D. is a clinical psychologist and sociologist, senior partner and director of Associates in Community Psychology—a clinical and consulting institute based in Alexandria, Virginia. She is on the Board of Directors of Sozialwissenschaftliches Institut fur Katastrophen und Umfallforschung in Kiel, West Germany, and does consulting on women in developing countries as well as consultant for local agencies serving women ex-offenders, battered wives and rape victims. She is affiliated with the D.C. Rape Crisis Center as a consulting psychologist and with the Center for Human Rights and Responsibilities in London, England.

Rona Fields was recently awarded recognition as a Founding Foremother by the Association for Women in Psychology and was also involved in the founding of Sociologists for Women in Society. She served on the first American Psychological Association Task Force on Women in 1970 and started teaching courses in women's studies at the inception of that discipline. She has been on the faculties of California State University, Los Angeles, Long Beach State University; California State University at Northridge, Pacific Oaks College, Pasadena City College, and Clark University. She has held adjunct professorships at American University and George Mason University.

In 1975, Dr. Fields was a Fellow at the Peace Research Institute of Oslo (Norway) and served as guest professor at several institutes affiliated with the University of Oslo at that time. She has guest lectured at universities in Ireland, England, Portugal, Israel and Lebanon, where she was guest lecturer in Sociology at American University of Beirut.

The author's publications include professional papers and articles in Psychology and Sociology journals here and abroad, chapters in several edited volumes, and the books *Society on the Run* (Penguin Ltd. 1973); *The Armed Forces, Movement and the Portuguese Revolution* (Praeger, 1976); *Society Under Siege* (Temple University Press, 1977) and *Northern Ireland* (Transaction/Society Books, 1980).

Rona Fields has been a free-lance correspondent for the Irish Press; the *Irish Independent,* Radio/Telfis/Eirean (RTE) all in Ireland, and has been affiliated with print and broadcast media in Los Angeles and Massachusetts.

Dedication

To Miriam Cathy Kate Kayla Sarah Jenny Natalie Emer and Granie Maeve Shiela Fiona Ann Dianne Carol and Dana and Ursula Denise Pam Ruth Lisa Luz Shirley Mary Maire Pauline Nancy Rose Trish Sattie and Peggy Margaret Ann Kathleen Barbara Patricia Marlene and Leda Esther Shulamith Judith Magda Jeanne Lora Rae Jessie Rita Dorothy Cheryl Lillian Bella Doris Ora Ofra Marsi Berit Karen Roberta Frances Louise Emma Helen — and Molly, of course, who says . . .

. . . I dont care what anybody says its much better for the world to be governed by the women in it you wouldnt see women going and killing one another and slaughtering when do you ever see women rolling around drunk like they do and gambling every penny they have and losing it on horses yes because a woman whatever she does knows where to stop sure they wouldnt be in the world at all only for us they dont know what it is to be a woman and a mother how could they where would they all be if they hadnt a mother to look after them. . . — Joyce, *Ulysses*

Contents

Preface

Earlier this evening I was talking with Rosa, who in addition to being many other kinds of person, is a woman in transition. She is in her late thirties; a mid-level civil servant on her way up to a senior executive position in the U.S. civil service; a widow; a child of immigrants; and a bilingual, bicultural new-middle-class person who jogs, rides horses, and does not know where she is going because she does not know what she "ought to want."

Tomorrow evening, I shall be seeing Rachel. She is twenty-two, the eldest of three lively, intelligent daughters of a mother in transition and a father who is, according to Rachel, "going nowhere." Her mother has just opened a one-woman show off Broadway, but to make her transition she has left home and spouse after long, frustrated years of housewifery and motherhood.

Richard wants an appointment with me. His wife and his sister have both been clients of mine as they have struggled with the role-model-less roles into which they have been cast. Richard's wife is now reading *The Women's Room* and telling him that he will never understand her nor really be involved in her struggle. He feels abused and alienated. He has been trying to establish a day-care facility in the new high-technology company where he works. The women he meets at work all feel that he is the one man they can talk to because he is not sexist. Why, then, he asks, is he so frustrated in his relationships with his wife and sister?

Ruth is currently enrolled in a course of study that will lead to certification as an engineer. She no longer feels that her value as a person is measured by success in the marriage market or that meeting men in school is the purpose of being there. She is not opposed to dating, but sexuality is not now a means for manipulating relationships. Most important, Ruth is beginning to realize that when important questions are asked, she is likely to know the correct answer because she is intelligent and has "done her homework." Relationships with women friends have taken on new meanings too. She no longer feels threatened or competitive with other women and has stopped thinking of her mother as a tragic, dependent person.

But, then there is Sharyn. Her father and mother "liberated" themselves from each other and decided that, having been parents until they were forty-five years old, they no longer had to perform that role. They were not

1

critical of the lesbianism of one daughter, the philanderings of their son, or Sharyn's promiscuity. Sharyn is convinced, however, that women are tramps and are not to be trusted, that men are valued, and that the two-month fetus she aborted was a son she murdered. She does not like herself and tries very hard to make me dislike her. She says she wants to marry and have children but that she will kill any girl infant. She says she wants to be a mother and a wife, but she has never really lived with either model. Her parents are multimillionaires, but Sharyn claims she has no place to live.

Joyce and Rebecca found each other in a halfway house for women ex-offenders. Rebecca was ostracized and castigated during her more than two years in prison because she is a "stud" — a gay woman who identifies as masculine. Joyce was accepted into the "sorority" house section of the prison because she is conventionally feminine in voice, gestures, and grooming. As black women they have experienced and witnessed sexual and racial exploitation and have never experienced paternal love any more than their mothers experienced human fulfillment. The counsellors at the halfway house are ambivalent about recognizing the relationship between Joyce and Rebecca, yet they know that neither woman has ever had a successful relationship with another human being. They want women to succeed in the real world when they are released from the program, but are afraid for them. If Joyce were to spurn Rebecca (and Joyce has a long trail of fickleness), would Rebecca return to heroin and the criminal activity that financed her drug habit? Just because a woman has been exploited and hurt by men, there is no assurance that she can relate successfully to another woman. As Rebecca points out, a "gay stud" is rejected as cruelly by other women as she is by heterosexual men.

It is not easy for someone who has been the target of discrimination, who has been ill used and oppressed, to be generous and kind, or to reach out to those less fortunate or in trouble. People who have been victimized tend to avoid taking risks. Transitional women have spent most of their lives struggling against victimization and are often deaf to cries for help from their sisters. Transitional women have been socialized to expect that they are in a competition for scarce resources and that it is "each woman for herself" (with a man for protection, if she is lucky and smart). Despite these warnings, women have begun to transcend both the fear of success and the fear of risk by accepting one another, however different from each other they may be.

For men who welcome these new women, there are joys beyond the pitfalls. For example, Richard does not have to meet the macho expectations his military officer father imposed on him as an adolescent and from which he rebelled. He has the freedom to be tender, and he is not expected to make all decisions and supply all financial resources. Also, he wants to experience parenting in the way his mother played that role, and he is not apprehensive about his unconventional aspirations. His wife, Laura, is a pianist, but she also shares in sanding floors while they renovate their house together.

These people are all friends and clients of mine. I am a psychologist, a university professor, the mother of young adults, a feminist, a social and political activist — and a woman in transition. This book is about all of us — Rosa, Rachel and her mother, Richard, Ruth, and the rest — and me. Although we range in age from 20 to 50, we are a transitional generation together. We have lived through the changeover (an international one), from women defined by their domestic relationship to a world in which many women have several alternatives from which to choose their identity.

We, the transitional women, bear the scars and experience the stings of remaining with one foot still on the old turf as we reach forward with the other foot, risking our balance and our survival. In this precarious state we often have only one another for support, but we sometimes glimpse the shape and color of that new ground. In this book I am trying to develop an idea of how that ground will feel, based on where we have been and what has been happening to us.

The idea for this book came, appropriately enough, while I was enroute to the Mid-Decade Conference on Women sponsored by the United Nations as part of its Decade on Women. I had been working with feminist and other women's groups throughout Western Europe, and to a lesser degree, Eastern Europe, because I was concerned that this opportunity to put a solid foundation under the new ground would be lost forever in the miasma of international bickerings about unsolvable problems. The Mid-Decade Conference had to transcend these clichés and constructively debate the status of more than half the world's population, women.

As I traveled and met with women I realized how desperately we needed to talk with one another and delineate our paths and objectives. The women I met were neither leading their governmental delegations as policy makers nor fully informed in advance of the agenda and procedures. If this was characteristic of the Western delegations, it was even more evident in Third World delegations. As I went from the UN sessions to the Forum and back again, I was at times hopeful and at times angry, often shocked, and during the last days intermittently bored and impatient. In the official meetings, one delegation after another presented synopses of changes and improvements in the status of women in their country. These reports were exciting.

They demonstrated that nations had been compelled to take seriously the issue of women's status and women's needs. Whether much or little had actually happened, the nations were being called to account.

But I was angry and horrified when women attacked other women — hurling insults and denying each other the right to speak. I was frightened and furious at the same time by the suspicions and inuendoes that had nothing to do with women's status and everything to do with intergovernmental feuds.

The final frustration was the embodiment of the others because the final document sacrificed unanimity of a program of action for women's equality. It produced yet another document adopted by a UN vote split on the basis of international bloc alliances and international politics rather than a shared commitment to women.

Like most events, however, a little distancing in time brings considerable objectivity. Some months later, I more carefully addressed myself to the documents that emanated from this conference. I also reviewed documents generated in the Forum prior to the conference and concluded that we really do have a strong new foundation in process. In 1973, at the First International Feminist Planning Conference, we were trying to chart the ways we would have to go to learn about, document, and change the conditions that diminish women. Today, seventy-three countries have signed the UN Convention on the Elimination of All Forms of Discrimination Against Women.

It is important in the light of these international decisions and plans to catch some glimpse of the lay of the land toward which we are moving. And so I am writing this book. We can know something of where we must go from understanding where we have been, and we can learn how to get there. This, then, is a guidebook to that place where the Future of Women is being made.

Chapter 1 TRANSITION: A CRITICAL TIME

There is an old cliché that you can view a glass as either half empty or half full. At this point in transition it is impossible for women to be certain whether the glass is being filled or whether the small amount that has accumulated in it is being drained.

If the twenty-first century is marked by the fact that technology will make women ideal employees and managers, there is still considerable evidence that attitudes as well as the existing structures mitigate against accepting women into the stratosphere of top-level decision making. Word processors are replacing typists and file clerks, and men are entering the secretarial workforce. With fancier titles and higher pay, men are using the new technology to expand and increase their productivity. And what about women?

Women's chores once were undertaken in a community of women — whether washing on the banks of a river or shopping daily for groceries in the marketplace. This community provided a network of support, as well as the reinforcement of social approbation. But the washing machine, vacuum cleaner, and refrigeration left women isolated and with higher standards for excellence in cleanliness and all other tasks.

Women have moved out of the old pattern of segregation from men and communion with one another into a tenuous integration between the sexes. Now these are enormous expectations for achievement — expectations by women themselves and imposed as a challenge to women by the institutions of Western society. Women, individually and as a group, have become "test cases" whether they are prime ministers of nations or the first women to work in a coal mine. There is a quality of heady exhilaration among women as they move to meet these challenges.

But there is a darker side to the new life of equalization. Statistics on American women show that working wives suffer stress-induced disorders and that as more women enter the workforce the morbidity and mortality statistics for women indicate significant increases in the incidence of anomalies previously considered "masculine." U.S. health officials estimate that now one in three Americans with a drinking problem is female, compared with one in six only a decade ago. The same proportions hold true for women involved with property crimes, such as embezzlement, fraud, and forgery. And although twice as many men as women kill themselves, would-be female suicides increasingly use historically male methods, such as hanging, gunshot wounds, and deliberate car crashes. Middle-aged working mothers, dissatisfied with clerical and sales jobs, are twice as likely to develop heart disease as are housewives, according to the U.S. Heart, Lung and Blood Institute. While the number of adult men who smoke has dropped, women have continued to smoke in the same percentages, and among teenagers, more females smoke than males. Fewer women suffer from depression, insomnia, and drug abuse than did a decade ago, but more women drivers are injured in car crashes. [1]

On a worldwide basis, the gap between the sexes in job efficiency and training has also increased as "women's tasks," such as water carrying, fuel gathering, and food-chain activities have been little influenced by technological advances. At the same time, throughout the world there is increased sharing of the role of breadwinner and no appreciable increase in sharing the role of child rearer.

More women are now in the workforce for a longer period of their adult lives. Despite laws that mandate equal opportunities and equal pay, women remain so far below men in earnings and status that men who have dropped out of secondary school earn more a year than women who are university graduates. Only one in ten female workers earns as much as a man would in a comparable job. [2] Even when men and women are paid equal starting salaries in technical and professional jobs, over a working lifetime (and in some cases within three years) the woman earns two-thirds to three-fourths the man's salary. Women, by and large, are not unionized workers and are often employed in undervalued occupations such as clerical and service jobs, nursing and health care, teaching, social work, and retail sales. The best job opportunities are in male-dominated fields like engineering, accounting, and computer technology. And when female-intensive jobs become valued and competitively paid, as some nursing specialties have become, men enter these fields too. Now that there are male flight attendants, regulations have been eased on height and weight, personal appearance, and marital status. This has been one job category where men have been dramatically freed to be employed in a remunerative career because women were made equal.

In many different ways, women's life-bearing function has been used as an excuse to keep them from full membership in society. Motherhood has been glorified on one level and trivialized on others. Although millions of fine words have been spoken and written concerning the primary role of women in rearing children, few societies have upgraded the low status accorded this activity. Looking after children — one's own or other people's — is traditionally "woman's work" and is therefore regarded as the natural corollary — some would say the price — of being born female.

In Western society particularly, there is generally little community support for the woman with young children. Usually financially dependent either on her partner or the state, she is likely to find herself marooned at home with the children, gazing at days of housework stretching ahead. Inadequate nursery school provision makes return to work difficult and jeopardizes any chance of engaging in nonchild-centered activity. Also, since the prevailing assumption still is that husband, home, and children should satisfy women's innermost longings, women frequently feel guilty when they experience discontent, boredom, or frustration. Voluntary work has helped many women retain a sense of independence, but work of this kind has been impossible for many others and has been regarded by not a few as a very flimsy palliative for an unsatisfactory situation.

The dream of the wife and mother at home, hardly visible among the roses and mounds of baking, is fading fast. But for many married women, this has not even been a dream. In many societies economic necessity has forced women to work in agriculture and industry. And such work has been in addition to bearing and rearing children and doing the domestic chores that are so necessary and so little valued. In the United Kingdom, more than half of all married women now under the age of sixty work in paid employment outside the home. In most cases this work is organized around the woman's domestic responsibilities and often involves caring and servicing activities similar to those she does in the home. The dual nature of many married women's work, and that of single women with dependents, has meant two things: (1) that all women's career opportunities are more limited than men's; and (2) that career opportunities for women who choose not to have children are also more limited than men's.

Although women's status has been laregely determined by social attitudes to marriage and childbearing and rearing, women's place in the broad social order also varies according to prevailing political and economic circumstances. In times of war, for example, women are commonly called upon to do jobs usually done by men — and when this happens, child-care facilities are instantly made available. In peacetime, the state and private employers are reluctant to offer such help. In pioneer societies, such as that of colonial America, women were respected as equal partners in the struggle for survival and were accepted in a wide variety of trades and occupations.

Women as a Minority Group

To suggest that half the world's population be regarded as a minority group may strike some readers as absurd. Today, however, a discussion of any minority group is likely to focus on underprivilege and lack of power rather than population statistics. The word "minority" is understood to imply not only smaller numbers but also less economic potential, fewer opportunities for social advancement, and less likelihood of being able to influence the dominant culture. In this context women may legitimately be referred to as a minority group.

In the economic sphere, women perform two-thirds of the world's total work hours, receive one-tenth of the world's income, and probably possess less than one-hundredth of world assets.[3] "Woman's work" is a phrase that universally implies dreary, repetitive, unremunerative labor. Comparatively few women, even in countries where they are nominally full citizens, have attained positions of responsibility in government, the professions, industry and business, and religious and cultural institutions.

Whether they go out — to work, to school, to the theater — or whether they remain at home — doing housework, caring for children, reading, watching television — female human beings are likely to be reminded fairly sharply, fairly often, that they are outsiders in a man's world.

The chapters that follow consider in more detail the nature and implications of this pseudo-minority status of women. Just as important, however, are the ways in which women are rejecting the assumptions that underline their minority status and are demanding a different future for themselves and the men with whom they must live and work.

The 1980 Mid-Decade Conference of the International Decade of Women, sponsored by the United Nations, revealed, as never before, how closely the status of women follows overall social and political trends. An examination of the reports supplied by member states of the UN suggested to me that the following principles operate across cultures and, to some extent, across history.

Women's position in any society is directly related to the social and political conditions of that society. If there is unrest, disorder, or distress in that society, it will affect women particularly harshly.

The status of women in a society is a function of that society's definition of marriage and family, which are themselves defined by childbearing and rearing practices.

There is no firm evidence that women as a class have ever enjoyed the prerogatives of power equally with men. Certainly, individual women have been accorded power, but only on the understanding that they will behave "like one of the boys."

In most countries throughout the centuries, rape, kidnapping, and enslavement have been used to control and terrorize women.

The denigration of women, like the denigration of a racial minority, provides an excuse and rationale for their economic exploitation. By assigning women an inferior status in the workforce, it is possible to get more work for less pay and to prevent the full employment of all workers, including men.

The subordination of women is worse within groups that are themselves oppressed. In such groups, when the man is forced into a subordinate relationship to other men and his masculinity is denied, he seeks masculine potency through sexual domination of the women in his group.

The more dependent a society is on the whims of fate and the natural environment, the more oppressed it is by mystic taboos which tend to polarize the roles of men and women and regulate relationships between them.

The status of women is adversely affected by wars and violence. Wars and violence glorify the stereotypical qualities of masculinity, but force women further into the role of breeder and feeder because the survival of the group is threatened. Furthermore, wars and violence require a psychological dehumanizing of the enemy and, in particular, of the women of the enemy society.

During the course of this book I examine many of these principles in greater detail, but for the moment, let us confine ourselves to the last point. It has often been argued that women's status generally improves in times of war — more women are drawn into the workforce and into unusual jobs, and more decision making devolves upon them. Such improvement is almost always ephemeral. When the crisis is over and servicemen become civilians again, women are ejected from the job market as rapidly as they were drafted into it. During the Second World War, for example, American and British women by the thousands left their homes and entered factories, offices, and government service to support the war effort. Many of the younger women among them were encouraged to envisage a future of productive and interesting work. But demobilization spelled an abrupt end to such hopes. The 1950s reinforced, blanket fashion, the image of woman as homemaker and mother.

Repeatedly, during wars and revolutions, women's nontraditional roles have looked like blossoming into an egalitarian society. Yet if one looks at the salient political crises of this country — at the Russian and Chinese revolutions and at the establishment of the State of Israel — it becomes clear that women revert to their subordinate status as soon as the crisis is over or at most within a decade.

What Women Have in Common

Although the position and experience of women depend largely on the society and class into which they are born, it is becoming increasingly possible to think, read, and write about a "female world." Instead of accepting the inevitability of being "the Other," as Simone de Beauvoir conceptualized the female sex in a male world, women are beginning to rediscover the virtually ignored part they have played in the world's history and to look forward to a future in which they are no longer mere appendages of men, the "second sex."

It may be useful to consider at a basic level just what women do have in common. Universally, they have conceived and borne children; they have provided the primary support and means of socialization for the helpless young in every society; they have shared the physical and psychological consequences of a complex, cyclical reproductive system; they have in the past, as today, carried out much of the work of the world for a small proportion of the world's income; in every society they have assumed responsibility for "invisible" and unpaid domestic work and for the nurturing and tending of other people. In most societies they have also been asked to believe that the male sex is naturally superior to their own and to make it their business to embody the often contradictory fantasies imposed on them by men trapped in male traditions.

Only very recently has female scholarship begun to provide information on, and analyses of, the "female world" — a sociological concept that implies the existence of, among other features, language, institutions, role relationships, customs, attitudes, expectations, and mores. Given the fundamental similarities in female life, it is not surprising that a female world embracing all these features can be shown to exist. But neither is it surprising that this world is only now being described and documented. After all, up to the present time, male authorities and male traditions have dominated the social sciences; as a result, questions and problems of interest to men have been pursued assiduously, while questions and problems of interest to women have rarely even been formulated.

Now, many academic disciplines are offering findings that challenge accepted views of the world. In anthropology, for example, female scholars have shown how one-sided field studies of preliterate human societies have been.[4] In history, women have found documents long neglected or ignored as trivial and have made visible trends and movements invisible to male-oriented historians. In economics, attention has been drawn to the way in which a whole area of work — domestic and subsistence work — has failed to be counted in the world's balance sheets.[5]

Studies of this kind are of vital importance not only to the integrity of the academic disciplines but to the social, economic, and development planning projects that make extensive use of theories and findings from the social sciences. Research has shown, for example, that the exportation of European male biases has in many ways seriously damaged development programs in the Third World. In one instance, because the European technical advisers assumed that men were naturally superior in the art of farming, they concentrated on teaching modern farming techniques to men. Since their wives were traditionally the cultivators, the men paid little attention to this unsolicited information, with the result that the women continued to do the farming using traditional methods and tools![6]

A clearer understanding of the real contribution to civilization made by women in the present and past is necessary if a brighter future is to be grasped. Traditionally, women have learned from men; it is now time for men to learn from women and their history.

Despite opposition and oppression, women have bonded and are bonding together to improve their position in society and bring about radical social changes. In nineteenth-century America, women's voluntary societies alleviated the harshest effects of rapid industrialization and urbanization; in nineteenth-century England, Elizabeth Fry and Florence Nightingale fought for and brought about lasting changes in prison and medical conditions; and in this century, women have spearheaded campaigns for world peace and international cooperation.

It is essential for the quality of future civilizations that women be able to take a full part in the running of their societies. Men, as well as women, stand to gain from this sharing of power, this living in an egalitarian society.

Men as individuals, apart from the sociopolitical concern for the status quo, have been manifesting transitional problems of their own. If women are not ready to go forward in their struggle for equality in tandem with men, the latter are even less prepared to enter that partnership themselves.

The media have been busily addressing the needs of women from the days when their major function was housekeeping and child care to the present "dress for success" fads. Men's needs, if any are recognized at all by the media, consist of *Playboy* sex and *Sports Afield.* Do men have needs, we might ask, apart from their physical condition? Their genitals and biceps would seem to be their definition.

Books that tell women how to be more like a man — when they purport to tell how to be assertive or successful or a winner — may be peddling archaic objectives and fantasies because for at least a decade, the leading male in films and novels has resembled Woody Allen more than John Wayne. The New Woman is not only victorious in the media but also much more adaptive to the requisites of everyday life in the modern world than is the hunter-warrior image that guides "masculinity." Warren Farrell's *The Liberated Man* argues persuasively that men are prisoners of their traditional social role and cannot be happy until they become more like women — androgynous.[7] As if to dramatize his point, we have rock stars like Mick Jagger and David Bowie — men who are frankly sensuous and somewhat effeminate (at least when contrasted with such predecessors as Elvis Presley and Jerry Lee Lewis).

Men today are suffering from "performance anxiety" that overflows basic sexuality to encompass efficacy on the job and in personal relationships. The competitive striving, aggressiveness-rewarding society stands in opposition to the increasingly bureaucratic style that characterizes postindustrial society. Service industries and managerial complexes do not provide tangible rewards or immediate feedback on performance that meets the "measurement criteria with which men seem to be born," says Kriegel in *On Men and Manhood.*[8]

Male bonding has been a function of basic masculine insecurity over their sex role. Margaret Mead has pointed out that men's sureness of their role is related to their ability to practice some activity that is exclusive to them as males. This, of course, relates back to the primitive recognition of the vital role of the female in the perpetuation and survival of the species and the estrangement the male experiences from these essential mysteries.[9] If women are permitted access to all places where men congregate and if women are allowed to perform the same functions, men who are still operating on a "measurement principle" will suffer severe psychosomatic consequences as well as extremely strained relationships.

But the man's problems do not end with his recognition of equality and acceptance of androgyny. There is the additional problem of defining what constitutes androgynous sharing. There is a very big difference between the equal sharing of housework and child care when both parents are employed and the assignment of tasks on some stereotypical baseline. If finding a babysitter or missing a day of work because a child is ill becomes the mother's assigned role, there is no new sharing. If the husband is presumed to be the carpenter/electrician for the household and is "given" housework assignments by his wife, there remains the asumption of difference. The woman and the man must be able to accept equivalence in the kitchen as well as at the workbench.

Ellen Goodman described the epitome of this transitional dilemma in a brief fantasy/analogy in her column reviewing Superman and Lois Lane in the film *Superman*. She described their inter-action as the "fatal attraction of the Semi-Liberated Lady for the Traditional Man who is Trying to Change." Goodman described Superman as a traditional man growing up on the ultimate "performance trip."

Women on Women

One reason for the transitional woman and the conflict entailed by her predicament is that a generation of women is reaching maturity in the 1980s that has been provided with many of the choices their mothers lacked. These younger women have graduated into a world of work and social circumstances that the previous generation struggled hard to open for women. But these women, and women who have lately gravitated to the women's movement, do not really comprehend the struggle required to make their new life style. Their current female role models are most often the well-tailored, conventionally mannered, successful women who are just a notch or two above them in status and years. They did not batter their bodies against the barriers; they moved cleanly into and through the breech. While they take for granted their opportunities in the workplace, they chafe at the "superwoman" model. Like the Israeli kibbutzniks who have never in their lives experienced the conflicts, crises, and problems that arise from the nuclear family life style their parents abolished, the young women of the 1980s want the fantasized romantic tradition. They often harbor resentment against the "abrasive" and "crude" mannerisms and strategies of the "breakthrough" generation. And for this reason the strategies and even the objectives of the women's movement have become a re-*action* instead of a re-*creation*. For younger women, established procedures and practices have considerable appeal. Their organizational style is no longer inconoclastic. But they do not realize that their societies have moved a far distance from the time of the hunter-warrior and that we have entered an era when the values, virtues, and uniqueness of women's culture is appropriate for progress and survival. It is impossible to turn back the clock. The liberation and equalization of women economically, politically, and socially has been as much a function of the social order in which it is taking place as it has been a product of the psychology of women. As other parts of the world move forward into less labor-intensive economic systems and provide a level of service predicated on increased education for all the population, they will also face the necessity for changed political, social, and male-female relationships.

It is not easy to be independent. Nor is it easy to accept the fact of choice and the responsibility for having made a decision.

Is Feminism the Answer?

The politics of feminism are unpopular because they require women's freedom and impose the responsibilities of that freedom. Simone de Beauvoir addressed this problem nearly thirty years after her landmark work, *The Second Sex*. She said, "I do not think women should take up power against men thinking they will be able to avoid what men did against women."[10] She saw power itself as the problem — not who holds the power. Feminism is a politics, and as the women's movement appears twenty years after its rebirth, feminism is being eliminated from it no differently than it was pushed out of the women's suffrage movement of an earlier era. If woman's oppression has had any effect on her positive qualities, de Beauvoir thinks it would be better to communicate these to men rather than suppress them among women by denying the experience. De Beauvoir views gender roles as social constructs, and views the institutions created and preserved through gender constructs as debilitating because of the limitations they impose on people.

There have been enormous changes in the numbers of women participating in the mainstream of economic and political life. Nevertheless, women remain the lowest-paid persons in the workforce, and are vastly underrepresented at the higher levels of the academy, business, and government. Women continue to face the pressure of having to do everything better to get half as far. And — for better and probably also for worse — new girl networks have replaced old boy networks in pursuit of economic and status prizes.

There is a chance that the new society toward which we are heading can be a more humane and personal one than before. If so, it will be a direct consequence of the equalization of status between men and women and because of the liberation of men and women from institutions that are no longer defined by current practices.

The Sexual Woman

Heterosexuality and sexual intercourse have become more androgynous. Women were not "liberated" by the sexual liberation movement, but they have become considerably more knowledgeable and articulate about sexuality, and probably more actively determine their sexual experiences.

Sexual liberation attempted to impose on women the reverse "oughts" of those under which they had been confined before. Previously, "nice" women didn't enjoy sex and would "submit" to their husbands when commanded. Sexual liberation ordered women to enjoy sex — frequent sexual intercourse with a variety of partners — and to take an active role in making themselves orgasmic. If the old system was oppressive, the sexually liberated model imposed oppression in combination with exploitation and an utter denial of individuality, choice, and personal integrity.

I started planning the curriculum for a course in human sexual behavior to be included among the offerings in a women's studies program when a troubled young freshman tearfully confided to me that she was "sexually perverse." Expecting that she, like some of her peers, was about to confess a lesbian preference, I said, "I doubt that you're perverse, but you may feel different. Why don't you tell me what you mean by 'perverse'?" She sobbed, "I'm still a virgin and I don't want to change that and I know that's wrong because I'm nineteen and no one else I know here is still a virgin!"

She was appealing to me to tell her how to stop wanting to be a virgin. I realized then that young women today are under enormous pressure to become objects of sexual exploitation — to a degree exceeding the pressures placed on turn-of-the century immigrant servant girls or eighteenth-century Pamelas. Now it is done on a rationalization of "mental health" or "liberation."

In the women's movement, sex for women has been redefined. The redefinition has much to do with women's struggles against rape and the traditional criminalization of the rape *victim* rather than the punishment of the *rapist*. It is also a consequence of the insistence by lesbian women that "man-defined woman" cannot be truly liberated. Heterosexual women took these cues and added to them findings about women's orgasmic potential to formulate a new ideology of female sexuality. Several of the most radical new ideas are that women's orgasmic potential is individual and different from that of men; that women obtain greater gratification when they are able to engage in the coital act more actively; that clitoral stimulation need not be gymnastically achieved but intercourse and male orgasm are not necessary for sexual gratification. After an exhaustive questionnaire survey of women's sexual behaviors and preferences, Shere Hite reported on data submitted by nearly 2000 American women. She concluded:

> Specifically, in sexual relations . . . we can . . . reopen many options. All the kinds of physical intimacy that were channelled into our once mechanical definition of sex can now be reallowed, and rediffused throughout our lives, including simple forms of touching and warm body contact. . . . Just as women described "arousal" as one of the best parts of sex, and just as they described closeness as the most pleasurable aspect of intercourse, so intense physical intimacy can be one of the most satisfying activities possible in and of itself.

> There is no reason why physical intimacy with men . . . should always consist of "foreplay" followed by intercourse and male orgasm. . . . You can have sex to orgasm, or not . . . genital sex or . . . physical intimacy. . . . There is never any reason to think the "goal" must be intercourse. . . . There is no standard of sexual performance . . . against which you must measure yourself; you aren't ruled by "hormones" or "biology."[11]

All of which has enormous implications for male liberation as well as the obvious fact that sexual intercourse can become more androgynous. As Rollo May, Marc Feigen Festeau, and others writing on masculinity assert, men have been denied the pleasure of feeling even to the extent of their expectation of intercourse. They have believed that the ultimate attainment of the act is the release of tension provided by the orgasm itself. They have been denied the pleasure of building up to orgasm or the desire itself even while they have been taught to prolong their erection. The measurement of performance value by which men determine their satisfaction denies any appreciation of the myriad human feelings experienced in desire and arousal, touching and kissing.

It may be that men and women are much more alike than either has been able to realize. The common humanity we share may finally be realized through the assertion of women's knowledge of themselves and the practical behaviors that result from their respect for their own integrity.

Notes

1. Joan Lublin, "Cost of Equality?" *Wall Street Journal,* 14 January 1980.
2. C. B. Lloyd, ed., *Sex, Discrimination and the Division of Labor* (New York: Columbia University Press, 1975).
3. International Labor Organization, *The Status of Women: Mid Decade* (report of the United Nations Mid-Decade Conference on the Status of Women, Copenhagen, 1980).
4. Ernestine Friedl, *Women and Men: An Anthropologist's View* (New York: Holt, Rinehart and Winston, 1975).
5. Cynthia Fuchs Epstein, *Woman's Place: Options and Limits in Professional Careers* (Los Angeles: University of California Press, 1970).
6. R. Dauber and M. Cain, eds., *Women and World Technological Change in Developing Countries* (Boulder, Colo.: Westview, 1981).
7. Warren Farrell, *The Liberated Man* (New York: Random House, 1975).
8. Leonard Kriegel, *On Men and Manhood* (New York: Hawthorn, 1979).
9. Margaret Mead, *Male and Female* (New York: Morrow, 1949).
10. Simone de Beauvoir, *The Second Sex* (New York: Knopf, 1949).
11. Shere Hite, *The Hite Report* (New York: Macmillan, 1976), 365.

Chapter **2**   WHERE DO WOMEN
COME FROM?

Woman's distinctions — which are remarkably distinguished from those of lower-primate females and more distinct from the human male than is the female of any other species — have made her The Mystery. In various cultural millieux and historical epochs, women have been associated with magic and superstition. The powers attributed to women are contradictory and extraordinary. Women have been thought to have the power to heal or harm; to bless or nurse; to nurture or kill. All these capacities are connected in the most primitive manifestations or the most sophisticated conceptualizations of the power of procreation.

Only in relatively recent times, and not even today throughout the world, have women realized that they can control their fertility. The power of procreation attributed to women has been based on deterministic and mechanistic beliefs. As recently and narrowly as women have realized their self-control, men and women have become aware that women do not control the sex of the offspring. In many societies women were believed to be the determining influence on whether sons were born. They were put aside or divorced if they were "unable" to bear a son.

The mystery of woman is celebrated in both the statue of Boadicea that stands beside the British Museum and the Marian theology of Roman Catholicism. The stories of Eve, Miriam, and Deborah that seem to contradict one another in Jewish scriptures have respective parallels in Shakespeare's Lady Macbeth, Portia, and Ophelia.

Universally and always, woman symbolizes the mystery of the life cycle. In every human society (and most animal societies, too), an infant's first knowledge of another human being is of the mother, who is, in effect, the infant's life support system. It is not surprising, then, that in many societies little boys try to emulate their mothers and assume that the female form is the ideal. The secondary sex characteristics of his mother (her breasts particularly) represent sustenance. The world into which the infant is thrust transmits through the relationship between infant and mother and the cultural coding of relationships between people, between the person and the natural environment, between persons of different status, and perhaps

18

most significantly, between males and females. There is currently strong evidence to suggest that even the birth experience itself imposes a cultural pattern on the new member.

Margaret Mead, the anthropologist who studied several remote societies and developed systematic approaches to comparing cultures, noted that the primary format of mother-child interaction determines the pattern of emotional relationships for that society. She categorized these patterns as "symmetrical," "complementary," and "reciprocal."

> To the extent that the child's whole individuality is emphasized, there is symmetry; to the extent that its weakness and helplessness are emphasized, there is complementary behavior; . . . to the extent that the mother gives not only her breast but milk, there is the beginning of reciprocity. But cultures differ greatly as to which they emphasize most.[1]

Passivity, competitive striving, or aggressiveness; an emphasis on monogamy, polygamy, or polyandry; practices of infanticide and female circumcision — are all based in and produce one or another pattern of priorities.

There are various cultural emphases on parts of the body, such as the mouth or the hands. In some societies, anthropologists tell us, such a strong focus is placed on teaching the young control of elimination that they later transfer this teaching to control of genitalia in the most restrictive fashion. For such groups, even legitimate sexuality may be a hasty, covert matter. Cutting across these concerns are the attitudes toward human dimorphism that determine relationships between the sexes. The prolonged helplessness of the human infant and the food ecology of the human species seem to have established the family as the basic social unit in every human group. The family is the legitimate unit for the indoctrination of the young into the ways of their society, although dimensions and descriptions of the family unit differ considerably from one culture to another and over history.

So, too, the institution of marriage varies from group to group and historically. Whatever its nature and longevity, however, marriage exists in some form in all societies, and all incorporate the incest taboo to varying degrees. Even in societies in which incest within a primary relationship was permitted, it was on the basis of superordinate status rather than the mental or physical condition of the pair. Thus, while marriage between first cousins was illegal in most of nineteenth-century Europe, the royal houses of England, Austria, Germany, Russia, France, Spain, and Greece incorporated many such marriages.

While the primary nurturing responsibility of the mother is consistent across cultures, her intimacy with the infant is closely shared by the father in some groups. In fact, the experience of pregnancy and childbirth is emulated through couvade by the men in some societies. Less directly imitative, but an almost universal substitute for woman's more obvious role in childbirth, is the male initiation ceremony. The basis for it is something like this: If only women can make babies, then only men can make men. Otherwise, the male's role in the basic mystery of life would be alienated. Whether the initiation into masculinity is through the sharing of secrets and blows, as in the Mundugamoor society, or through intoning a portion of the religious scripture, as a Jewish boy does at age thirteen, this masculine ritual symbolizes the male giving birth.

The folk tradition of woman as the harbinger of death is personified in the Irish tradition of the *banshee*. Women of several family names or clans were believed to have the capacity to foretell the death of someone. They would keen, or wail, just before the death occurred — even if the dying person was nowhere in the neighborhood. Along with this keening, or just preceding it, the banshee (Literally translated, the "woman fairy") would "see" the person who was about to die. Moreover, such clairvoyance was believed to descend through the women of certain families as a kind of inherited trait.

In most of the world's religions there is a relationship between the female goddess and death. In Christianity, the Pièta, or mourning mother of Christ, cradles the son she brought into the world. Because of the high infant mortality rate of every generation up to contemporary Western society, a mother often cradled a dead infant or child she had borne. Female saints were often in their lifetimes practitioners of the healing arts and caretakers of the dead.

Kali, the Hindu goddess of death, is also the earth goddess and the goddess of light. In this respect, she shares in the mystery of the three capacities of the Hebrew moon/female. The ancient Greek goddess Hera was celebrated as wife and mother but was destructive and killed even her own son. The mythological mature woman/mother figure was viewed in many cultures as nurturant and dominating but because of this power, as potentially devouring and castrating.

In the ancient world of Greek mythology, this conflictual omnipotence of the female was somewhat conciliated through the myth of the Amazons. Their name comes from the Greek "without breasts" because they supposedly cut off their right breasts in order to facilitate drawing the bow. There is no certainty that such a group ever existed, but the idea of an all-female society in which men were used for sexual gratification but male infants were killed at birth was perpetuated in other times and cultures with certain consistent features. These women were warriors, often successful but ultimately defeated by great heroes, each of whom finally had to test their strength against them. Herodotus related that the demise of the Amazons came about through their yielding to the Scythians, with whom they preferred sex to victory. Gaelic mythology similarly presented the Danum, who were skilled practitioners of the martial arts residing in Alba (Scotland) and were the teachers of the great warrior hero of Ulster, Cuchulain.

In Sparta and Lesbos, during the Archaic period, women achieved the sexual and intellectual equality reflected in the works of Sappho. (Sappho was born into an aristocratic family in Lesbos around 612 B.C. Lesbos at that time was known for its acceptance of male and female bisexuality and for its eroticism.) The Athenian lawmaker Solon institutionalized for Greek, and later for Roman, society the dichotomy between women as respectable and women as whores. Solon's legislation, which minutely regulated Athenian life, was predicated on keeping women from becoming sources of friction between men. This legislation initiated the dichotomization of sexuality.[2]

Life and death, religion and power — these are themes and institutions universally and historically rife with sex-role prescriptions and attributions. More than perhaps any other aspect of society, control of the mysteries of life and death combines with the mysteries of female cyclic bleeding and pregnancy. Out of ignorance and powerlessness comes the idea of woman as witch or goddess, as saint or seductress. Ancient religions and even contemporary Judaism and Christianity reflect many of these concepts and continue these primitive explanations of the universe. Often in Western society such religio-cultural ideas persist in popular literature and the media. One such notion is of the moon as female and as representative of femininity and procreation. Jewish literature identifies the moon with women, with the promise of redemption to women. In many societies, as well as in Jewish religious culture, the new moon represents the monthly physical renewal of women and is usually a cause for differentiation in rituals and other behaviors.

Culture and Women or Women's Culture?

In all the discussions about how women got where they are, there is the nature versus nurture argument. One side says that women are the way they are because of the way they are made; the other side insists that women's place and history have been determined by cultural surroundings and that societies have placed women in restricted roles and have limited their access to power. There may be a third approach to the question, and while it does not eliminate the stronger arguments for either position, it may present a more consistent perspective for examining women's status and history. The alternative is women's culture.

The criteria for identifying a culture include a value system, language, institutions, role relationships, customs, beliefs, and mores. This seems to be a very complex context in which to place persons as different from one another as Sappho and the contemporary grade school teacher, but all women share much in common. Women universally and historically have borne children and have been the primary support and socialization system for the helpless young; they have shared the physical consequences of a cyclical process that signals their fertile years; and they have been the invisible and unpaid workers and primary agents in the caretaking of other people. Even women's language is different from that of men. In almost every language group — there are a very few interesting exceptions — the social roles described through masculine nouns and power behaviors described through masculine verbs exclude women and even imply subordination and oppression. Women's identification with the weak and vulnerable combined with their nurturance and early expectations of nurturant behaviors produce a different perspective on relationships between the powerful and the helpless. In some circumstances this perspective even translates into ideological and political differences between men and women. This distinction is at times evidenced in the roles women take in contemporary Western society, but it is succinctly articulated in the classic Greek play *Lysistrata*. The drama shows the cultural antagonism between women as social conservators, life-bringing and life-sustaining beings, and men as warrior-competitors. The idea of women's antagonism to war and their refusal to provide sexuality for warrior societies exemplified in *Lysistrata* was invoked by both American and British women in the suffrage movement during World War I, and by the Scandinavian Women for Peace at the UN Mid-Decade Year of Women Conference. Women as peacemakers is another phenomenon that argues the existence of a women's culture. Yet, women as heads of governments have not been notably more pacific then men. Indira Gandhi, Golda Meir, and Margaret Thatcher have not acted to end all military actions by their governments. At the same time, one cannot point to a woman Minister of War or Defense, and whatever the society's attitude toward military service for women, rarely are women placed in a combat role.

Pre-Christian Celtic women were equal warriors with their men. Boadicea led her people into battle against the invading Romans. And by virtue of their service in combat, women were accorded equal property rights under Brehon law. Seventh-century Christianity in Ireland changed that by imposing fines on men who endangered a woman's life or were responsible for her death. Thus women could no longer be placed in combat. At the same time, rights to property in the clan and to positions of leadership remained the prerogative of warriors — thus excluding women.

Studies of lower animals have suggested that differences in the brain and central nervous system functioning of male and female animals result in different responses to stimuli. We know, however, that the mediating function of the brain is more extensive and complex in humans than in lower animals and that the brain and central nervous system are more responsive to hormonal influences in lower animals than in humans. If the findings of differential response programs are applicable to humans, then women would be culturally bonded as a consequence of biological patterning. Even if there are no biological bases to brain response differences, there are differences between human males and females in the rate of psychoneurological development, which would provide cultural differences to some degree. Whether through early attention and training or because of hormonal activity, directional orientation and fine motor coordination develop more rapidly in girls than in boys. Because they have a greater attention span and more manipulative ability, girls learn to read and write at an earlier age than boys and are less likely to have speech and language problems than boys. Girls become more focused on verbal interchange and on interpersonal relationships through communication. The earlier initiation of puberty in girls may also have implications for cultural differences between the sexes.

Bonding itself is an indication of cultural relatedness. Female apes bond and thus often serve as substitute mothers for each other's offspring and as "aunts" in the socialization of the group young.

Bonding in human males has been remarked upon as a particularly masculine propensity. Teamwork has been emphasized in male socialization throughout most societies as requisite for accomplishing "male tasks," such as hunting, warfare, and sociopolitical functions in the form of religious ceremonies and governance. Less frequently emphasized but equally pervasive is the male competitive striving, which extends even to mate selection. In contrast, competition in mating behavior is often cited as characteristic of a woman's individualism and her unsuitability for team efforts.

Arguments about female competition in the marriage market may be quickly countered with reference to all the polygamous societies in which women share a single man and form a society of women among themselves. In contrast, there are very few known polyandrous societies, and the most prominent of them consists of men who are biological brothers sharing the same "wife." Thus competitive mate selection arguments rebound more to the discredit of theories about masculine bonding behavior than to refute the existence of women's culture.

Cultural Determination

Marriage and the family are as much the basis for understanding the cultural determination of women's status, role, and predicament as is women's culture. The family system defines women's economic relationship with the larger society and is an expression of the socially organized productive cycle.

While the mating process embodies the cultural values and dynamics of any social group, for women in every society, their relationship with that process serves as their definition and social position. One example of this is the way a woman's title, unlike a man's, differs in accordance with her marital status.

In most societies, woman's work is housework and child care, tasks that are unpaid and outside the socially organized productive cycle. Therefore, it is not socially valued work. In this framework, women are dependent for survival first on their parents and then on their mates. In the late seventeenth century, women's role was so circumscribed by marriage and domestic requirements that J. Richards, an author of the time whose manuscript now reposes in the British Museum, described women as "these miserable creatures, who have no other knowledge than that they were made for the use of man."

Women were not rewarded for being anything other than creatures for "the use of man," and women of learning and wit often were made to suffer for their accomplishments. The few women of achievement who survived adverse reactions usually were forgotten by biographers and historians unless they were married to, or close kin to, a famous man. Yet women in Europe continued to become scholars and healers and some women in the otherwise repressive eighteenth century owned shops and pursued businesses and trades.

In England, and often in France as well, women who violated their status as subordinate wives or daughters were punished in the criminal justice system more severely than were men. Even today, a woman convicted of killing a brutish husband or lover out of jealousy or fear is sentenced more heavily than the man who kills a faithless wife or her lover.

When a woman chose to, or was compelled to, separate her sexual life from the institution of marriage by having a child out of wedlock or becoming a prostitute, her status became further denigrated. The men through whom the lower status was conferred experienced no equivalent denigration. Even in more enlightened recent times, in Europe and America, when attention has focused on pregnancy or childbirth out of wedlock, the focus of the social scientist and social and legal agencies has been on the mother — the woman — and not on the father of the infant. Similarly, prostitutes are charged with morals violations, but rarely are their customers or their pimps confronted by the legal code, or the social researchers' questions.

Today, in many parts of the world women's wages and social security benefits are controlled by their husbands. More than two thousand years after Solon's legal system deprived women of property rights, married women remain the property of their husbands. Single women are the property of their fathers almost as much in Dublin as in Riyadh or Buenos Aires.

Women's socialization into a narrow range of roles is so related to the marriage and child-rearing practices of a society that in the few historical or contemporary instances in which there is no such thing as "illegitimate birth," women have achieved property rights, participated in the productive labor force, and contributed to the intellectual and economic life of the society at large. We can compare, for instance, the eighteenth-century teenager who bore an illegitimate child and was thereafter a social outcast with the fourth-century Celtic woman for whom every relationship with a man had some legal status, and who maintained the right (until her child reached the age of forty) to "name" the father, and by virtue of the nature of their relationship at the time the child was conceived, to correctly anticipate shared responsibility in the child's care and upbringing. Even the child of a slave had legitimacy and a socially acceptable role in society.

Currently, in societies where women have increased access to paid employment and have chosen to pursue careers, they have fewer children and take the initiative in contraception. One may argue whether the change in the economic sphere preceded the change in orientation toward family size or whether improved contraception freed women to increase their participation in the marketplace, but there is a remarkable change concomitant with the change in the socialization of little girls. This is in itself a cogent argument for viewing women's condition as a product of cultural imposition.

Fate and Taboos

Women are more mysterious and potentially evil when people are less in control of their fate. Xenophobia, the fear of outsiders, is a common reaction among groups or nations when their security is threatened or otherwise unstable. For men, who usually have held the political power of groups and nations, women may be viewed as "outsiders" especially because of the mysteries surrounding their menstrual cycle and the process of procreation. During the Middle Ages and in the seventeenth and eighteenth centuries, women were accused of witchcraft and put to death as mass hysteria followed upon some natural disaster or a threatened social or political change. In a less cataclysmic manner, wives were discarded for failing to "produce a male heir," as if by their malevolent magic the chromosomes had not matched up to the sovereign's order.

In times when men who communicated with deities were revered as prophets and sages, women were regarded as sorceresses for the same behavior. Contemporary psychoanalytic interpretations of this phenomenon put the blame on men's fears of castration and their need to demonstrate their prowess in the face of the unknown. By denying women access to power through every vestige of the political ordering, the threat of their "magic" is allayed.

Women are, universally and historically, subordinated and restricted in their behavioral possibilities and their choice of life patterns and pursuits. Nonetheless, women are the basic socializing force and sustaining influence on the very young. This paradox has resulted in the emergence of an identifiable and universal "women's culture" and the cultural delineation of woman's place as determined through childbearing and child-rearing practices. Woman's power and mystery are feared and celebrated, but finally and firmly in every society, they present a challenge to masculinity.

Notes

1. Margaret Mead, *Male and Female* (New York: Macmillan, 1949), 65.
2. Elizabeth Gould Davis, *The First Sex* (New York: Viking Penguin, 1979).

Chapter 3

INSIDE A WOMAN'S HEAD

Twelve years ago, I attended a scientific meeting for psychologists who specialize in developing techniques for changing behavior. Their branch of psychology, known as behavior modification, may be applied to change the behavior of the old or the young, the normal or the disturbed — indeed any branch of society that is deemed "changeworthy." One of the speakers, an expert in devising sophisticated equipment and techniques for the purpose of behavior change, described a mobile learning center for children. This center could be put up next to a police station and would link in the minds of the young the pleasure of learning and the work of the police. The idea struck me as pretty bad, but there was worse to come. The speaker went on to describe some machinery he and his colleagues had created to magnify sensory information beyond normal levels. The part that dealt with sound sensations was in the form of a Picasso-esque woman with knobs fashioned as breasts and the motor sited roughly where the uterus would be. He proudly described this as an "asthetic advance" in practical design.

After his presentation, I could hardly wait to express my outrage at this travesty on woman. As I waited my turn to ask a question and listened to the questions raised by my colleagues, male and female, and all students or professors of psychology, I realized that the machine-woman did not seem out of place to them. No one else seemed to resent the image of manipulating a woman through her sexuality.

Twelve years ago we were living in a world that had no qualms about manipulating people, particularly women, through their sexuality. The period of transition from a sexist to an egalitarian society had just begun. Certainly the nonsexist outlook had scarcely impinged on woman as portrayed by psychology. Let us focus on scientific psychology's view of the female psyche prior to the shock waves of feminist thinking, and go on to ask where this view came from and how it is being modified in this period of transition. After all, the future of women depends not only on economic and technological advances but also on how women as individuals see and understand themselves.

Psychology is concerned with understanding the human mind and human behavior. Psychologists have emphasized in particular two interrelated areas relevant to the status of women: the differences between normal men and women in their basic thought processes; and the problems that characterize women who suffer from "psychological distrurbance" – women who are "mad."

Traditional Psychology and Women

As far as basic psychological processes are concerned, psychology's traditional view of woman mirrored commonly held beliefs. In the intellectual sphere, evidence was collected (selected?) to support the belief that women are superior to men in verbal skills (they have a better command of language), and men are superior to women in spatial and mathematical skills (they are more skilled at manipulating shapes and numbers).[1] In the sphere of personality and emotion, studies both in the West and cross-culturally supported the belief that women are less aggressive, more passive, more dependent, more easily upset, and more prone to emotional expression than men.[2]

Overall, then, women were seen by psychology as the weaker sex. Women were therefore regarded as more prone to "psychological disturbance" than men.

Where did this sexist picture of women come from? The answer is not difficult to find. Since most psychology prior to the 1960s and 1970s was done by men, the areas singled out for investigation, the methodology used, and the theories that emerged all had a strong masculine bias.

Mainstream psychology and psychiatry have not been noted for an open-door policy toward women. This is a legacy from the medical profession. In late nineteenth-century Europe and America, when psychology and psychiatry were becoming specializations, there were formidable barriers against academic training for women. Nevertheless, a few women slipped through the net of prejudice. Helen Thompson Woolley, who was granted a philosophy degree from the University of Chicago in 1903, was the first woman in America to complete a graduate program in psychology. She went on to make important contributions in the field of child development. But she was an exception. Other early women contributors to psychology suffered considerable humiliation in their pursuit of doctorates. Mary Calkins was denied a degree for her work at Harvard, and Christine Ladd-Franklin was refused a degree at Johns Hopkins University after presenting her thesis. (Incidentally, the first women to attend classes at John Hopkins had to sit behind a screen![3])

During these early years, psychology in America was largely an academic discipline, not an applied one, and hard as it was for women to matriculate through the institutions of higher education, it was harder still for them to obtain teaching posts. Many early women psychologists pursued their careers in the then new women's colleges, and few had access to research funds, modern facilities, or support staffs. In consequence, they had little opportunity for research or extensive publishing.

Women who did receive training in psychology and related disciplines tended to channel their energies into reform movements and into working with children and social outcasts. In their research and clinical work with these people, they did not meet the same roadblocks that beset them in other specializations within psychology. The stereotyping that associates women with the nurturance of the weak and unfortunate actually worked in their favor! They turned this small area of advantage into a power base within psychology. But until the emergence of child guidance clinics, in which women developed new roles, techniques, and approaches for psychology as a whole, psychology was not really a practical discipline. Insofar as it was practical, it was intimately linked with medicine and psychiatry, both bastions of male privilege.

Women's contributions to psychology must be viewed against the backdrop of power brokers, such as G. Stanley Hall, the founder of the American Psychological Association and of Clark University. Although Hall instigated research into child development, juvenile delinquency, and learning, he was strongly opposed to the involvement of women in psychology — or any other branch of academe. Clark University, of which he was founder/president, did not admit women students until after World War II, and even recently has been found guilty of sex discrimination by federal agencies. Hall proclaimed that women who eschewed marriage in favor of a job were selfishly violating their biological capacity; they were damaging their gynecological functions and their personality. Hall's views, and those of his colleages in the new American psychology, were consistent with those of Freud and Jung, both of them psychiatrists who viewed psychological sex differences as having biological causes.[4] One does not have to fantasize a conspiracy against women to recognize that a science that excludes half the human race from its practice can hardly sustain a scientific perspective on humankind.

The area of educational testing provides one example of how American male psychologists misused psychological tools to ensure that the profession remained male dominated. The techniques of educational testing were devised by female psychologists, but since the 1950s they have been used to justify professional discrimination against women.

Educational testing procedures are widely used to assess the relative potential of candidates for a range of postgraduate programs and professional work, such as psychology and law. Testing is based on the premise that given a written multiple-choice test in a large, formal, and controlled environment, the responses selected by the candidates will indicate their suitability for the proposed work. Different tests are used to assess candidates' suitability for different professions, but this basic procedure is common to all such tests.

Since places in clinical (that is, applied) psychology programs have always been limited by the amount of supervision needed, this specialty has tended to rely very heavily for its choice of students on the results of such testing. In fact, an early study (1955) showed clearly that in tests requiring qualitative responses, women and sensitive men performed significantly less well in a large, formal testing environment than in small classroom situations.[5] This discovery led to no change in the testing arrangements favored by the university administrators. As a result, the intake of students for clinical psychology programs continued to be composed mainly of the least sensitive male candidates.

Reverberations from the decision to ignore uncomfortable evidence are not confined to the field of clinical psychology. Community psychology, or community mental health, was a discipline pioneered in the United States by female psychologists, many of whom had not taken part in clinical graduate programs at the doctoral level. In the early 1960s, when a considerable amount of federal funding was made available to establish and extend this new discipline, the graduate schools of psychology began to take a belated interest in the new field. They instituted programs for training in community mental health – and systematically adopted the same kind of educational tests for candidates that had previously been shown to discriminate against women. By the 1970s women had become a minority in a field that, like clinical psychology, was dominated by men – and probably by men who scored low on measures of sensitivity.

Prejudice against women in psychology went beyond personal humiliation and disappointment for the women concerned. It led, in effect, to the evolution of a male-biased subject. Supposedly masculine psychological characteristics (aggression, dominance, and leadership) were favored areas of study; male bias even encouraged a preference for using men rather than women as research subjects. Consequently, the accumulating body of knowledge was based on studies conducted by males on males engaged in male pursuits. Most of psychology has been about men, not women.

The one area of psychology that cannot be accused of male bias in its data base is the psychoanalytic movement. Sigmund Freud, the father of psychoanalysis, developed his theories from case studies of patients who were, in the main, neurotic women. Indeed, most of Freud's clinical experience was with female patients. Yet he produced a far more detailed and coherent theory of male psychological development than of female. Take that well-known chestnut, the "Oedipus complex." Freud argued that a boy, somewhere around the age of five, is in love with his mother and fears that his rival, his father, will cut off his penis as punishment (the "castration complex"). The only solution for the boy is to try to be as much like his father as he can. Indeed, Freud believed that is through identification with the same-sexed parent that children acquire a sexual identity and a moral sense.[6]

What about the girl? She, like the boy, is in love with her mother, but this love soon turns to hate when she realizes that her mother, like herself, is without a penis. The girl discovers that women do not have this momentous organ, and so she identifies with her father, who does. For the rest of her life she is plagued with a desire to possess a penis ("penis envy"), but the nearest she will ever get to satisfying this desire is to have a baby (Freud saw babies as penis substitutes), preferably a boy baby. So girls do not achieve a satisfactory resolution of the Oedipus conflict, which means, according to Freud, that women never achieve as fully developed a superego, or moral sense, as men.

Freud thus gave pseudoscientific credence to the stereotype of woman as an overgrown child. No wonder he has been the target of concerted feminist attack. In her book *Psychoanalysis and Feminism,* Juliet Mitchell provides a detailed account of how feminist theorists have debunked Freud.[7] (In fairness to Freud, it should be noted that several distinguished feminist scholars, including Juliet Mitchell, have argued that Freudian psychoanalysis can be seen to offer a useful way of understanding sexual development as a social process.)

Most feminist scholars have pointed out that, taken at face value, Freud's statements about women are patently unsatisfactory. The problem, they argue, is not that women fail to grow up but that Freud was so blinkered by his patriarchal viewpoint that he failed miserably in his attempt to understand women. It was up to the few women who did manage to enter the inner sanctum of psychoanalytic theory and practice to try to set the record straight.

Karen Horney, born in Hamburg in 1885, became a member of the teaching staff at the newly founded Berlin Psychoanalytic Institute in 1920.

Three years later, she published the first of a series of papers on the psychology of women.[8] Her life and work exemplify how closely a theorist's personal circumstances dictate lines of scientific inquiry. Because of the differences between her own life and the lives of her male colleagues, Horney began to analyze the impact of culture on individuals, regardless of sex. In doing so she argued against the Freudian concepts of penis envy and female masochism built on by many of Freud's disciplines, including Helene Deutsch (her psychoanalytic interpretation of women was published as *The Psychology of Women* in 1944).[9] Long before it was recognized as such, Karen Horney developed an analytic perspective that was androgynous, without diminishing the essential distinctions between the male and female psychocultural experience. Her position is summarized in the following statement from her paper "The Dread of Woman," published in 1932:

> Now one of the exigencies of the biological difference between the sexes is this: that the man is actually obliged to go on proving his manhood to the woman. There is no analogous necessity for her; even if she is frigid, she can engage in sexual intercourse and conceive and bear a child. She performs her part by merely *being,* without any *doing,* a fact that has always filled men with admiration and resentment. The man, on the other hand, has to *do* something in order to fulfill himself. The idea of "efficiency" is a typical masculine idea.[10]

Perhaps the relative obscurity of Horney's thinking, at least until the recent resurgence of feminism, reflected the fact that her contribution to personality theory was consistently presented in textbooks only as a postscript to Freudian theses. The work of Clara Thompson, who followed in Horney's footsteps and laid the groundwork for the development of psychiatric social work, integrating the individual, the family, and the society in the therapeutic process, was not widely recognized either.

Frieda Fromm-Reichman, another psychoanalytic theorist and writer, elaborated and dissected Harry Stack Sullivan's theory of interpersonal relations, and came to the conclusion that any social system that accords status differentials on the basis of gender is inherently pathological. This insight, too, went largely unnoticed.

The originality, and indeed the optimism, of these early psychoanalytic nonconformists stemmed from their realization that sex-role aspirations and stereotyped behaviors are neither necessary nor biologically destined;

they are socially imposed and can therefore be socially excised. "Penis envy," "castration complex," and "infantilization" are concepts imposed on the adult woman; they are not facts of biology.

A straightforwardly Freudian approach is no longer the norm for psychoanalysts, but Freud's biological determinism underpins some of the most widely recognized and respected approaches to education, child guidance, child rearing, and clinical evaluation in psychiatry. Consider, for example, this description by the psychoanalyst Erik Erikson of the psychosexual problems of school-age children:

> Girls often have a difficult time at this stage because they observe sooner or later that, although locomotor, mental and social assertiveness is increased equally with, and is as adequate as, that of boys, thus permitting them to become perfect tomboys, they lack one item: the penis! and with it the important prerogatives in some cultures and classes. While the boy has this visible, erectable and comprehensible organ to which he can attach dreams of . . . adult bigness, the girl's clitoris only poorly sustains dreams of sexual equality. She does not even have breasts . . . her maternal drives are relegated to play fantasy or baby tending . . . where mothers dominate households the boy can develop a sense of inadequacy . . . the girl and the boy are now extraordinarily appreciative of any . . . promise of the fact that some day they will be as good as father or mother. . . .[11]

Note that it is the girls who have the biological problem — no penis — and the boys who have the environmental problem — feelings of inadequacy in the face of a dominant mother. The penis-centered environment that schoolgirls and adult women are subjected to seems to have escaped Erikson's attention!

During the first half of the twentieth century, in complete contrast to psychoanalytic explanations of human behavior with their emphasis on unconscious mechanisms and instinctual drives, the behaviorist school of psychology became firmly established. My antagonist of twelve years ago, the psychotechnologist with his machine-woman, was a product of this theoretical movement.

Behaviorism regards human development in general and the development of personality in particular as a series of learning experiences. We "learn" when external events and our reactions to them become associated, or "conditioned." For a behaviorist, differences between the male and female psyche are more a matter of learning than biology. Sometimes the learning process goes wrong, resulting in psychological disturbance, and then the individual must be redirected onto the right path by what is essentially a relearning process.

Behaviorism neglects the importance of people's thoughts and feelings; it regards human beings as machines capable of being prodded into action by events outside them. This simplistic view fails to capture the complexity and subtlety of the human psyche, but even though the theory has been challenged, the therapeutic techniques derived from behaviorism are still in use. Behaviorism has its own form of psychotherapy, called behavior therapy, which aims to do just this. The behavior therapist controls external events ("stimuli"), and provides rewards and punishments calculated to remove socially unacceptable behaviors ("responses") and shape new ones. "Desirable" behavior patterns are rewarded by positive reinforcements, and "undesirable" actions or activities are punished by negative reinforcements.

So, a woman patient who happens to have acquired behavior patterns inconsistent with prevailing role norms for women is taught a new set of behaviors, which conform more closely with those norms. She is rewarded for visiting the hairdresser or wearing a pretty dress; she is punished, usually by loss of privileges, if she indulges in unladylike behavior such as swearing or telling smutty jokes. Most of this therapy is conducted in psychiatric hospitals, of course. Where the relationship is between client and therapist, rather than between patient and therapist, the "reinforcements," or rewards, for socially acceptable behavior are rather less crude. Nevertheless, the basic function of behavior therapy is to change a person's behavior so that it conforms with stereotypes as interpreted by the therapist.

Perhaps the most questionable area of behavior therapy is gender identity training. This usually forms part of psychotherapy programs designed to help transsexuals adapt to the opposite-sex role. Transsexuals of both sexes are encouraged to acquire the stereotypical behavior of the sex they wish to adopt.

Another form of behavior therapy, "modeling," is nothing more than the application of a process that goes on from birth: the imitation of people or actions we admire. Teachers are expected to provide appropriate role models for the children they teach. A male teacher is expected to be aggressive, highly rational, knowledgeable about the use of tools, good at organizing things, and good at competitive sports. The female teacher as a role model is expected to be warm, accepting, conventional, and nurturant — in other words, she is a pseudo mother. Modeling, either as a deliberate form of therapy or in the normal course of education, results in nonstereotypical behavior becoming more unacceptable. Indeed, it is one of the machanisms of stereotyping in the first place.

The use of women as "wife surrogates" is also questionable. Sex therapy today is based largely on theoretical principles derived from the behaviorist school, and the function of the surrogate female sex partner is to provide reinforcements that will enable the "sexually inadequate male" to perform an "adequate" sex act. The role of such women is, in effect, no different from that of the courtesan or prostitute. In fact, during their research in the 1960s, Masters and Johnson hired prostitutes. Behavior therapy applied to sexual problems reinforces extant sex-role models. Nevertheless, there is good reason to believe that sexual inadequacy is a product of pathological sex-role stereotyping and that treatment, in order to be effective, must eliminate the specious barriers and limitations that stereotypes impose on human relationships.

Another theoretical framework that has had great influence on psychology's view of women derives from humanistic philosophy. This is a world view that states that everyone is potentially good and self-sufficient; if they are not, they have in some way been deprived of the opportunity for growth and development. This is in sharp contrast to the psychoanalytic view, which describes the new infant as "polymorphous perverse" or "seeking sexual gratification through all orifices," and to the behaviorist view, which supposes that the infant is a *tabula rasa* (blank slate) on which experience carves its likeness. A humanistic philosophy should, on the face of it, provide an agreeable and enlightened alternative to the dark closet of stereotypes in which the human female has been imprisoned. Unfortunately, it sanctions a rather subtlier interpretation of stereotypes instead of their elimination.

Abraham Maslow, the standard-bearer of the humanistic movement in psychology, developed a hierarchical model of the process of realizing human potential. A number of basic biophysiological or material needs, such as food, sex, and security, must be satisfied before higher order needs, such as justice, beauty, and wholeness, can be realized. This whole growth process is called "self-actualization":

> Self-actualization is not altogether general, it takes place via *femaleness or maleness,* which are prepotent to general humanness . . . one must first be a healthy femaleness — fulfilled woman — or maleness — fulfilled man — before general human self-actualization becomes possible. There is also a little evidence that different constitutional types actualize themselves in somewhat different ways because they have different inner selves to actualize.[12] (Italics mine.)

So the humanistic perspective includes the idea that women are "by nature" nurturant and have the need to "mother." It also supposes that female sexuality is a prerequisite to self-actualization as a woman and that if that sexuality is not fulfilled by nurturing or childbearing, it must be experienced vicariously through "a feminine occupation." The stereotypes are still there.

The unavoidable conclusion that must be drawn from these considerations of the foundations of modern psychology is that men have created a male psychology and have imposed it on women.

As early as 1910, Helen Thompson Woolley recognized the problems inherent in psychology as a result of its male orientation. She wrote scathingly: "There is perhaps no field aspiring to be scientific where flagrant personal bias, logic martyred in the cause of supporting a prejudice, unfounded assertions, and even sentimental rot and drivel, have run riot to such an extent as here."[13]

Is this still true? Men have created a male world for women to live in, but women are beginning to challenge patriarchy on all fronts, and psychology is no exception. The last decade has been a transitional era for psychology with more and more women not only entering the field but persevering to doctoral level to make substantial theoretical and research contributions. Women psychologists are challenging the old male-based theories and views of the female psyche. The male myths are being exposed. We now have a different and hopefully much more accurate view of woman, one in which the overwhelming importance of the role of socially imposed sex-role stereotyping has at least been recognized.

A Revised Psychology

Until 1970, psychology was guilty of adopting and perpetuating the belief that women differ fundamentally from men in terms of basic psychological processes. Yet, when the evidence came to be examined closely, these differences proved remarkably hard to pin down. Data relating to sex differences in psychological processes have been meticulously reviewed by two eminent women psychologists, Eleanor Maccoby and Carole Nagy-Jacklin, in their book *The Psychology of Sex Differences.*[14]

After reviewing all the literature on the development of perception, learning, and memory in infants, they concluded that no differences at birth can be reliably attributed to the sex of the infant. There is some reason to believe that female infants may be more sensitive to taste and smell cues and that their responses may vary more than those of male babies, but the evidence is not conclusive. They also found little evidence to substantiate theories of differences in the sensory orientation of male and female infants, or in responses to social and nonsocial stimuli.

The more important sex difference, the one difference of which psychologists were always so certain, concerned intellectual abilities. Women and girls, the assumption went, have superior verbal abilities, whereas men and boys have superior spatial abilities. This tidy assumption is no longer valid. Certainly no biological basis for such a difference has been identified. No straightforward relationship has been found between these abilities and sex hormones, or genes, or the structure and development of the brain. This absence of biological evidence has led psychologists to take a closer and more critical look at the original measures that claimed to distinguish between spatial and verbal skills. It is now considered extremely difficult, if not impossible, to devise tests that can with any certainty measure verbal or spatial ability as such. Tests always seem to involve a combination of the two abilities, and those that demonstrated apparent differences between men and women may have done so on some basis other than verbal and spatial abilities. It is important in this context to remember that all psychological tests involve evaluating learned behaviors rather than pristine, innate capacities.

We are left with no clear picture of how a woman's basic psychological processes differ from those of a man, if indeed they do. This does not mean that there are no important psychological sex differences; it means only that we have not found any that we can accept with confidence. In the realm of psychological disturbance, however, there are real and provable differences, and the insidious workings of sex-role stereotyping are a very probable explanation of them.

Madness: Male and Female

The unvarnished facts about women and mental health are these: More women than men receive psychiatric treatment of all kinds. Such treatment ranges from informal advice for emotional problems given by general practitioners to full-blown inpatient treatment for schizophrenic breakdown. The disorder in which the female-male ratio is most unbalanced is depression. Depressed women patients outnumber depressed male patients by about two to one in most industrialized countries. (An important result of this, incidentally, is that more women than men are likely to experience ECT (electro-convulsive shock therapy), a "therapy" found to permanently damage the brain and learning process.[15]

How are these remarkably clear-cut sex differences to be explained? There is a great deal of evidence to suggest that they reflect, not differences in basic psychological processes, but pressures to conform to the idealized images we have of women and men.

When people behave in ways that lead them to be labeled "mad," they are in fact behaving in ways that deviate from social norms. No behavior is in itself "mad." Everything depends on the expectations of the society concerned. We in the West put people in mental hospitals if they say they keep hearing voices; other societies regard voices in the head as a rare and valuable gift.

The increasing involvement of women in psychology has led to an awareness of the part that social expectations about sex roles play in the etiology of "madness." To what extent, it is being asked, can madness be understood as a failure to conform to sex roles?

Given the blanket imposition of rigid sex-role expectations on children in our society, it is somewhat puzzling that madness is not more common. There is considerable evidence, too, that the sex-role straitjacket is more constricting for girls than for boys. Many little girls are popped into dresses that require physical restraint and decorum if they are not to split at the seams and reveal more than they conceal. Though capable of excellent big-muscle coordination, most little girls are discouraged from displaying it — that would be unladylike and immodest. From a purely developmental standpoint, it is a miracle that little girls manage to develop such a high level of fine motor coordination when they are denied the use, and thus the development, of their larger muscles. Conversely, the socially imposed emphasis on robust muscular behavior for boys puts them at a disadvantage when it comes to the psychomotor coordination necessary for reading and writing in their early years at school.

Such inequities are continually carried forward and compounded during a child's development. Because of the greater decorum imposed on them, girls are allowed, even expected, to excel boys in early school performance when the criteria for excellence are good classroom behavior and verbal fluency. But by the age of twelve, girls learn that academic excellence is not the path to social success and, more painfully, that academic excellence to the point of superiority may leave them without boy friends, that most important symbol of adolescence.

One of the first pieces of research to seriously implicate sex-role expectations in madness was the famous study by Broverman and her colleagues in 1972.[16] They asked practicing clinicians to describe the characteristics of "the healthy adult male," "the healthy adult female," and "the healthy adult" (sex unspecified). The results revealed that clinicians have different stereotypes for "healthy" women and "healthy" men. Women are seen as warm and expressive, whereas men are seen as competent. The really interesting finding is that clinicians' descriptions of "the healthy adult" are much more similar to their descriptions of the "healthy" male than the "healthy" female. In other words, characteristics of the healthy female, while conforming to social expectations about women, are nevertheless regarded as less healthy than those of the healthy male.

So women are in a tails-you-lose-heads-I-win situation right from the start. The characteristics that society expects women to display are also those that society is liable to condemn. Add to this society's disapproval of women who fail to toe the sex-role expectation line, and one wonders how any woman avoids hospitalization. There are, of course, two extremes of failure to conform to sex-role expectations: overconformity and cross-conformity. For women, overconformity means extreme passivity and dependence (depression?); cross-conformity means aggressiveness and overt sexuality (schizophrenia?), or behaving more in accordance with expectations for the opposite sex role. Men, too, are labeled "mad" if they overconform to their sex role. Extreme aggression is regarded as psychopathic; but cross-conformity, or too close an approximation to the female sex role, is not tolerated either. But women have to contend with being regarded by clinicians as *by definition* less healthy than men, even if they show no signs of deviating from their stereotypical sex role. They are regarded as intrinsically more "mad" than men, a remarkable state of affairs that is discussed in detail by the American psychologist Phyllis Chesler in her book *Women and Madness.*[17]

How has this state of affairs come about? There are several possible reasons why more women than men are labeled "mad," but none of them provides a convincing alternative to the conclusion that women's madness has been to a large extent manufactured by patriarchal oppression.

One explanation is that women are more ready to report psychological distress than men. They actually may experience more psychological distress, but a more likely reason is that they are more prepared to admit it. Such an admission conforms to the stereotype of the "weaker" sex. Conversely, men are inhibited from reporting symptoms, for it is unmanly to complain.

Another possibility is that women are subjected to more stressful lives and therefore are more vulnerable to mental and physical illness. The stressors, or events causing stress, could be biological or social or both. Indeed, the complex female reproductive system has been singled out *ad nauseam* as the origin of most female problems. Man cannot be accused of postpartum or menopausal depression. Nevertheless, it is impossible to separate biological stresses associated with events like childbirth or the change of life from social stresses, and so a purely biological explanation of these depressions is neither accurate nor justifiable.

The psychiatrist Pauline Bart, for one, has put forward a social explanation of depression in women of menopausal age that fits the facts as plausibly as biological theories. At this juncture in her life, Bart argues, a woman may feel bitterly resentful at having devoted her life to mothering, only to find herself on the scrap heap when her children leave home. For their sake she may have endured the humiliation of an unfaithful husband, who clearly communicated his lack of sexual attraction for her, or the physical dangers of living with a violent spouse. Her anger at what she now sees as a wasted life may produce intense guilt because it implies a rejection of motherhood; this guilt may turn inward and result in depression.[18]

In addition to stress that may be related, for social or biological reasons, to her reproductive capacity, a woman may experience stress from being pressured into playing too many roles. Women today not only have to be attractive sexual partners and caring mothers but reliable contributors to the family income as well. Perhaps women are being asked to do too much. If the same were demanded of men, would they crack under the strain? We simply do not know. But we do know that the stresses set up by being expected to fulfill multiple roles are yet another example of how women's "madness" is linked with sex roles.

Careful scrutiny of the link between sex-role expectations and mental illness reveals that the female sex role is incompatible with health and stability. Sex roles are predominantly socially determined, as we know from studies of other societies. In our patriarchal society, therefore, we are forced to conclude that the imposition of unhealthy sex-role expectations on women by men is one of their most powerful and successful means of oppression.

The traditional clinical view that masculine health is the ideal for adult mental health is reflected in the recent popularity of "assertiveness training." Seminars, workshops, and management training programs encourage upwardly mobile women to abandon some of the characteristics associated with the feminine role and take on others commonly associated with the masculine role. Often the underlying assumption is that masculine assertiveness is the fuel that drives corporate wheels and that women's learned propensity to listen rather than talk, to ask rather than instruct, is a disadvantage in pursuing a high-level career.

At worst, assertiveness training can reinforce the view that the path to equality lies in women being pseudo men, with all the stereotypical masculine faults and deficiencies. If carefully and thoughtfully used, however, certain types of assertiveness training can help free women from their image of themselves as helpless and passive. Being assertive is not necessarily the same as being aggressive. For example, it requires assertiveness to say no to a request, to ask a favor, to initiate or terminate a conversation, and to express both positive and negative feelings. The best way to ask a favor is probably not to shout, and if you tell someone how much you like them in a harsh voice, you will probably not convey what you intended. At its best, assertiveness training aims to fill gaps in women's social skills, both verbal (what to say) and nonverbal (how to say it), so that they can be more effective in expressing their needs and feelings.

A Future Psychology of Women

From these arguments it would seem that the solution to women's "madness" is to change sex-role expectations. If there were no rigid prescriptions as to how the behavior of women and men should differ, there would be no norm to which people could be accused of over- or underconforming. This belief lies at the heart of Sandra Bem's research on androgyny. Bem has proposed that to speak of "opposite sex roles" is all wrong.[19] People are not *either* masculine *or* feminine in their personalities; rather, they can have masculine and feminine personality characteristics simultaneously. In other words, people can be androgynous. Bem has developed a questionnaire to measure the extent to which an individual is characterized by both masculine and feminine personality traits, and her research suggests that people who are androgynous have higher self-esteem and are generally better adjusted than people who are rigidly sex typed.

This is a strange claim in view of the fact that we so obviously live in a society in which there are differences in the qualities considered desirable and appropriate for each sex. Women fix dinners, while men fix cars; it is not expected that both fix both. But we must not overlook the fact that we also live in a society that values independence and self-sufficiency and that it is hard to be independent or self-sufficient if you are totally incapable of behaving in ways generally seen as typifying the other sex. Women who are able to display masculine as well as feminine personality characteristics and behaviors are going to escape the long arm of oppression.

As Bem has pointed out, the concept of androgyny has built-in obsolescence. If the ultimate aim is to create a world with no sex-role stereotypes, the concept of androgyny will become meaningless once this aim has been realized. In a totally androgynous society, it will be impossible to classify any characteristic as male or female. Obviously we have a long way to go before we achieve "the obsolescence of androgyny." But it is unfortunate that the idea of androgyny endorses the distinction between masculine and feminine traits; this is why many feminists treat the concept with a fair amount of skepticism. So, while there are signs that androgyny may become obsolete before it becomes obsolescent in Bem's sense, it has nevertheless been an important staging point in psychology's increasing understanding of the significance of sex roles for mental health.

The growing involvement of women in psychology has brought about a number of changes of approach to treating psychological disorders. Not so long ago, psychotherapy was a predominantly male preserve, with a clear difference in status between the male therapist and the female client and a general lack of sensitivity to imposed sex roles as major culprits in psychological problems. Women have done more than revise psychological theories and research; they have revolutionized their application.

"Feminist therapy" is not a shorthand for a specific technique or approach to treatment; it does denote a blending of traditional methods with a feminist perspective on mental health. Feminist therapy can be seen as having two, not always integrated, branches. One is, in the widest sense, political; it is concerned with changing society, nothing less. The other is more personal and is concerned with changing the individual. Given that much of women's "madness" may be rooted in sex-role stereotyping, the political branch is concerned with eradicating women's "madness" by eradicating sex-role stereotypes; it encourages men and women to work for social change, for a more equal society in which neither women nor men are squeezed into narrow norms. Tremendously important as such a long-term, global goal is, it is clearly irrelevant to a severely depressed and suicidal housewife; telling her she is the victim of society's oppressive sex-role system will not help her. So feminist therapy must also work at the individual level. Here its chief advantage over traditional techniques has been to stress a nonauthoritarian and egalitarian relationship between client and therapist. Women help each other in a warm and intimate relationship in which therapeutic techniques are totally demystified.

As a process intended to change the way the person thinks of herself, feminist therapy emphasizes the individual as a choosing being who can construct and impose a meaning and organization on disparate events, thus organizing and defining herself. The woman (or, in some cases, man) is encouraged to consider her past behavior and experience in the light of the dominant framework of sex-role expectations. Instead of blaming mother, father, or grandparents for adult difficulties in behavior and for feelings of helplessness, the woman is encouraged to see such difficulties as products of sex-role socialization — and, as such, as difficulties within her power to resolve. The process of therapy provides a new view of herself as an active and controlling being and contributes insights into how feelings can be redirected and behavior changed.

Through two clients of mine, each of whom I undertook to counsel during 1969, I first learned the real significance and application of feminist therapy. One was a young man, age twenty-one, who had just returned from combat duty in Southeast Asia. The other was a woman nearing forty, who was suffering from migraine headaches and colitis. At the time, she was studying to become an opera singer and was working for a behavior therapist as a "wife surrogate" for impotent men.

The young man's symptoms were sexual impotence and an extraordinary overreaction to being physically close to women; in these circumstances, he was completely incompetent in tasks he otherwise did well. Since his work was selling and repairing office machines, Bob was in serious trouble when he first came to see me. There was neither time nor money for extensive psychoanalytic studies of his early childhood. We needed to change his behavior as quickly as possible, and at the same time try to gain insight into the psychodynamics of his sexual dysfunctions.

At first he was a little annoyed that I did not want to hear about how his grandmother dominated his early life and about his alienation from his parents. But I did find of interest the fact that his first heterosexual experience to orgasm was with a prostitute in Saigon and that sexuality thus existed, from the age of eighteen, as separate in his life from any other functions and as a primitive act committed on the body of a creature scorned. When Bob returned from the war, he found that while he could talk with his American hometown white girl friend, he could not begin any sexual activity and have an erection. The situation worsened and began to affect his worklife. If he tried to work on a typewriter at the desk of the secretary who used the machine, he suffered tremors, sweats, and flushes.

Bob was the epitome of a man who viewed women as sex objects — and sex objects, moreover, who came from a conquered (or otherwise victim) people. For him, sexuality was separated from feelings, indeed from common humanity. As the vicious cycle of his anxiety escalated, his impotence with American women extended by association to incompetence when in the company of such women.

To help Bob overcome these crippling problems, I used the psycho-therapeutic techniques of desensitization therapy and stress reduction, in association with talk therapy designed to help him achieve a new orientation toward sex roles and identity. Although a man was the subject of this therapeutic process, the procedures and framework used were indisputably those of feminist therapy.

My woman client, Leonora, knew a great deal about the life of woman as sex object. Every time she had sought psychotherapy she had ended up either as mistress to the therapist or, as now, was hired to be a professional sex object. Not surprisingly, she was nonorgasmic. This fact had so intrigued all her previously male therapists that they had neglected to focus on the other 95 percent of her.

For a time, I too missed the central issue. As the therapy progressed, however, it became clear that her colitis, migraine headaches, and general malaise were associated not with confusion and unhappiness at being a high-class prostitute but with uneasiness that she actually enjoyed that life but felt that it was not right for her to do so. Long before she worked as a wife surrogate, and even while she was doing that, she was mistress to several wealthy men, who supported her in grand style while she surreptitiously read Marx and Engels and fantasized herself in the vanguard of antiwar protest marches. Since my own life and political line were somewhere near her fantasy life, she had sought me out as a therapist.

We soon established a good relationship. In effect, she taught me how to feel happy about charging a fee for my service; while, through me, she learned that it is more important to feel good about yourself than to measure and judge yourself by stereotypes and symbols. She realized, too, that she had very real control over her life and that she could achieve her emotional satisfactions without manipulating other people but through a genuine concern for their well-being.

Some Conclusions

Girl babies are not psychologically different from boy babies, but in the process of growing up, girls are constrained to behave in limiting ways that are not expected of boys. These constraints and limitations, and the self-concepts they engender, result in a self-fulfilling prophecy. Women become less able to be independent, less achievement-oriented, less rational, and more angry. Until recently, if they recognized anger and sought psycho-therapy, they often faced a psychotherapy that replaced the "gilded cage" with a steel trap.

Until the demands made by women in psychology and psychiatry compelled these professions to reexamine their premises, psychotherapy or hospital treatment for women's distress did not provide alternatives but imposed a system for reestablishing the constraints. By the time the nascent women's movement began to affect psychology, the ultimate applications of psychotherapy through psychotechnology were directed discriminately to women. Electroconvulsive shock treatment was most often administered to women, and these women were committed for hospitalization by their husbands.[20] Women were declared the better subjects for lobotomies; black women were described as the best prospects. Walter Freeman, the foremost proponent of psychosurgery in the United States, said:

> We vividly recall a negress of gigantic proportions who for years was confined to a strongroom at St. Elizabeth's Hospital . . . for [the] operation five attendants were required to restrain her while the nurse gave her the hypodermic. . . . From the day after the operation . . . we could playfully grab Oretha by the throat, twist her arm, tickle her ribs and slap her behind without eliciting anything more than a wide grin or a hoarse chuckle.[21]

Gradually the bases of psychological theory changed, and the practice of psychotherapy was amended. Feminist psychotherapy became a recognized alternative approach intended to fill the interval between the casting off of the evil old ways and the evolution of a new, nonsexist therapy. In 1978, Paula Caplan, a psychologist at the Toronto Family Court Clinic, presented her findings to the American Psychological Association annual convention on Erikson's thesis that boys and girls do not experience the world in the same way.

Erikson had theorized inner and outer space perspectives from the differences between the configurations constructed by boys and girls, aged eleven to thirteen, when asked to construct an imaginary scene. The boys built towers, and the girls enclosed spaces. Caplan found that Erikson's findings were a result of the toys he used, and the fact that the preadolescent children deliberately selected toys that were appropriate to sex-role stereotyping. When all children were given the same items, there were the same number of towers built by girls as by boys.[22]

On the other hand, newer and more sophisticated techniques for studying the brain have provided evidence that sex differences in cognition do not increase with age, thus suggesting that there are biological differences. Karl Pribram, a noted brain researcher, contends that these sex differences are a function of differing ratios of sex hormones acting on particular brain structures. From studies by Pribram and Dianne McGuinness we learn that that males function better at tasks in which the two hemispheres of the brain are not in competition, while females are better able to shift from one hemisphere to the other. At the same time, behaviors would affect the development of particular parts of the brain, and thus the big-muscle activity of boys would enhance adjustment to sudden shifts in visual environment, while the girl's activity in speaking and touching would enhance development of brain areas controlling dexterity and auditory sensitivity.[23]

A New Reality

There is no doubt that the science of psychology and the practice of psychotherapy have greatly influenced the social systems and life styles of people during the greater part of the twentieth century. Educational systems and vocational planning are based on psychology. In many countries, social planning is effected through the findings of psychologists. Certainly many social control and socialization process are formulated on the real or supposed knowledge of human nature currently dominated by the findings of psychologists. For evidence of ubiquity, one has only to survey the popular media to be confronted by the citations, quotations, and direct observations of experts on the human psyche.

Changes in the attitudes and proclamations of mental health professionals on sex differences are likely to receive attention and action. A major change already in evidence is the change in career/vocational expectations of boys and girls and a new emphasis on providing boys and girls equally with skills appropriate to their talents for the labor market and for personal development. Boys are now included in cooking classes, and girls are getting a chance at varsity athletic competitions.

New psychotherapies are providing support for women in transition. This is the generation that is feeling the real tension of the changeover. As Marya Mannes said in the 1960s when women were beginning to assert their ambitions for equality, "Nobody objects to a woman's being a good writer or sculptor or geneticist, if she still manages to be a good wife, a good mother, good-looking, good-tempered, well-dressed, well-groomed and unaggressive." This is the generation of the "superwomen," who are now beginning to rebel against that circumstance. And it may be the essential beginning to a breakthrough for the attitude born of relief that each person, man and woman, must exert the options and take the alternatives most suited to the individual self, without regard to traditional roles or expectancies.

It is very hard to be a pioneer — to lack authoritative role models. In this chaos, the mental health professional's task is to facilitate the weeding out of irrelevant compunctions and destructive behaviors that are the residue of preparation for sex-role behaviors that are no longer necessary and are often inappropriate. Women must become comfortable with making decisions, competing for first place, and actively determining their marital and familial status. In every society that equalizes women's work opportunities, there is a decrease in population growth. Women who make decisions in the larger world are also inclined to take decisive action about the use of their bodies for breeding.

One of the most urgent tasks for the mental health professional in this generation of mature men and women is to facilitate the new androgyny. Men need help to realize that they can express their emotions in tender ways and can enjoy parenting or nurturance. Women need to recognize that they do not have to lose the femininity they value in order to succeed in the boardroom. Psychologists in personnel and human resources development work need to contribute to changes in the workplace and work process from their new knowledge of sex differences.

But the beginning, like all beginnings, is the hardest.

Notes

1. E. S. Maccoby and C. N. Jacklin, *The Psychology of Sex Differences* (Stanford: Stanford University Press, 1974).
2. Ibid.
3. N. F. Russo and A. N. O'Connell, "Models from Our Past: Psychology's Foremothers," *Psychology of Women Quarterly* (1980): 11-54.
4. EEOC finding of probable cause on five counts of sex discrimination in *Fields* v. *Clark University,* 1979.
5. Cited in the *Report of the Task Force on the Status of Women in Psychology,* quoted in *American Psychologist* 28 (1978): 611-16.
6. Sigmund Freud, *Three Essays on Sexuality* (London: Hogarth Press 1905).
7. Juliet Mitchell, *Psychoanalysis and Feminism* (New York: Viking Penguin 1975), 303-50
8. Karen Horney, *Feminine Psychology* (New York: Norton, 1967).
9. Helene Deutsch, *The Psychology of Women* (New York: Grune and Stratton, 1945).
10. Karen Horney, "The Dread of Women," in *Psychoanalysis and Women,* ed. J. B. Miller (New York: Viking Penguin, 1973).
11. Erik Erikson, *Identity and the Life Cycle* (New York: Norton 1968).

12. Abraham Maslow, *Towards a Psychology of Being* (Princeton, N.J.: Van Nostrand, 1962).
13. Helen Thompson Woolley, *Psychology Bulletin,* 1910.
14. Maccoby and Jacklin, *Psychology of Sex Differences.*
15. Alan W. Sheflin and Edward M. Opton, Jr., *The Mind Manipulators,* (New York and London: Paddington Press, 1978).
16. I. K. Broverman et. al., "Sex Role Stereotypes: A Current Appraisal" *Journal of Social Issues* 28, no. 2 (1972): 59-78.
17. Phyllis Chesler, *Women and Madness* (Garden City, N.Y.: Doubleday, 1972).
18. Pauline Bart, *Sexism and Social Science: From the Gilded Cage to the Iron Cage* (Pittsburgh: KNOW, monograph, 1970).
19. Sandra Bem, "Probing the Promise of Androgyny," in *Beyond Sex Role Stereotypes,* ed. A. G. Kaplan and J. P. Bean (Boston: Little, Brown, 1976), 47-62.
20. Sheflin and Opton, *Mind Manipulators.*
21. Walter Freeman and James Watt, *Psychosurgery in the Treatment of Mental Disorders and Incurable Pain.*
22. Vivian Gornick, "Watch Out: Your Brain May Be Used Against You," *Ms.,* June 1982.
23. Ibid.

Chapter 4

WOMAN TALK:
LANGUAGE AND LITERATURE

The political status of women and the nature of women's culture are made manifest in language and serve toward sex-role socialization and self-image through literature. Languages reflect the values and practices of their societies, and in turn shape the practices and policies of these societies. A society's language encodes common values just as its economic system reinforces the values of that society. Thus, there are many differences, historically and cross-culturally, in gender usage. Studies by Jerome Kagan of Harvard University suggest that by the age of six, American children have assigned unspoken gender identification to even inanimate objects and have done so on the basis of the gender of the person associated with their use.[1] This is all the more a reflection of the way language reflects values when you consider that English, unlike French or German, does not assign gender to inanimate objects routinely.

The ancient Gaelic language, from which Irish and Scottish derived, did not incorporate into its grammar gender differentiations. And as we have noted, there were no significant differences between men and women politically or economically in Gaelic society.

The opposite was true for the ancient Hebrews. Gender identity conferred differences in every aspect of life, although the differences were probably not intended to signify inequality. One indication of this, say contemporary scholars, is that in every description of God the euphemism for the Name is described by both male and female adjectives and adverbs. This is supposed to indicate the universality of God's nature and power, as well as to equalize the values of female and male qualities. Moreover, each of the virtues described in Hebrew has a counterpart virtue, which is named opposite the sex of the first. That is, the virtues are distributed equally between masculine and feminine nouns and are not specific to males or females. For example, the word for "charity" is feminine, but all persons are required to grant it.[2]

There are and have been societies in which there are separate languages for men and women. In Japanese, little boys, along with little girls and women, use the female particles until the age of five. Some groups in the

Pacific Islands have language and language rituals exclusive to initiated males in the society; so, too, did some American Indian cultures.

Earlier societies actually had separate languages for men and women. The Carib, an ethnic group native to the western hemisphere before the arrival of the Europeans, was such a society. The Caribs were invading the islands of the Caribbean at about the same time as the first Spaniard expeditions. They came from South America and were cannibal warriors who ate their male enemies and captured the females for slaves.

These captives were Arawak women; they were peaceful, agrarian, and creative. Their submission to the Carib men was anathema to them, and in revenge they refused to learn Carib and continued to converse in Arawak. The men then considered Arawak a "female language" and refused to learn it. As the Arawak women were assimilated into the society, their language became the language of Carib women. Thus began the women's practice of speaking their "secret language."[3]

It is worth noting that even in this situation of exclusion from the secrets of half the society, the men considered this other language beneath their dignity. It was inferior because it belonged to women!

The Druze, in an opposite example, have a custom that emphasizes woman talk. When a Druze woman dies, all the village women gather together to literally sing her praises with epic poems and prose tributes. Only women participate; they never communicate to men the words they have pronounced with one another.

Living language is dynamic rather than static; it changes along with the society in which it used. One need think only of the new words and usages recorded in revised editions of dictionaries to realize that new concepts and inventions insist on being named and thus recognized. Similarly, the style and conventions of language change according to the particular society's habits and needs. Twentieth-century readers of English, for example, typically have a wide range of distractions and pressures in their lives; accordingly, on the whole they use a simple, direct prose style. Their eighteenth- and nineteenth-century counterparts had the leisure to fully appreciate an intricate, convoluted style of writing.

The relationship between changes in language and changes in social mores is by no means a simple one, which is perhaps why many people fail to notice it. For one thing, the mainstream use of language tends to enshrine conventional and traditional values and thus to lag behind social changes. Frequently, new words and usages are common currency in subcultures long before they attain general acceptability; "gay" instead of "homosexual" or "black" instead of "negro" are some examples. A related factor is that, even if subconsciously, most people realize that language not only reflects society's value and ideas but also plays an active part in shaping such values. Thus, the introduction of the word "black" to replace "negro" encouraged a move toward regarding people of Afro-American descent as equal in every way to white citizens. The word "black" is not merely the equivalent to the word "white." Language in a real sense constitutes power — the power of naming — and thus it defines the nature and potential of individuals and groups.

In societies in which English is used, the masculine viewpoint has been accredited with ultimate authority. Not surprisingly, therefore, the language reflects and encourages this bias through a wide range of linguistic and literary conventions. It is worth noting in this connection that although English teems with words (many of them abusive) for women and black people, only recently has a word been coined to describe, as it were, the standard product. "WASP" is a breakdown of White-Anglo-Saxon-Protestant and marks an attempt to show that the seemingly godlike anonymity of much cultural utterance is dangerously deceptive, for it masks particular interests and sets of values.

The contemporary Western women's movement has recognized the important role of language in reinforcing and encouraging prejudice against women and female achievements. During the last decade, female scholars have researched how language is used to denigrate women and explored how women themselves use language. Writers Casey Miller and Kate Swift have commented that "only recently have we become aware that conventional English usage, including the generic use of masculine-gender words, often obscures the actions, the contributions, and sometimes the very presence of women. Turning our backs on that insight is an option, but it is an option like teaching children the world is flat."[4]

What the authors mean by "the generic use of masculine-gender words" is the linguistic convention that in certain contexts "man," "mankind," and "he" refer not only to male human beings but to all human beings. For example, the British Broadcasting Corporation gave a major series on human evolution the title "The Making of Mankind." Studies have shown that usage of this kind tends, not unexpectedly, to suggest images of males only, not of females and males together. And indeed the writers who set out to use these words in a generic way often seem to confuse themselves by the end of their sentences. For example, Miller and Swift gave an extract from a magazine article in which "man" was used in its generic sense to imply the inclusion of women. By the end of the article, in a rather surprising volte face, the author wrote: "Man can do several things which the animal cannot do. . . . Eventually, his vital interests are not only life, access to females, etc., but also values, symbols, institutions."[5]

Frequently, use of the generic "man" is not so much confusing as actually misleading, inasmuch as the reader may automatically assume that "man" refers only to a male. English is, after all, unusual among European languages in that its assignment of gender is not "grammatical" but "natural." In other words, three categories — feminine, masculine, and neuter — are applied, respectively, to female creatures, male creatures, and things that have no sex. In languages such as French and German, masculine and feminine genders are assigned to inanimate objects as well as to living things. The reader of English, therefore, may expect a male noun or male pronoun to refer only to a masculine person. Miller and Swift provide a fine example of how language can help women in public office achieve instant oblivion: "In reporting the remark of a member of Congress, 'Every man in this subcommittee is for public works,' the *Wall Street Journal* appended a comment, 'There are two women on the subcommittee, and they are for public works, too.'"[6]

Two points can be made about the generic-use phenomenon, which continues to plague the English language. One is that such usage perpetuates the idea of female human beings as a kind of subspecies. The other is that terms such as "man" and "he" are *false* generics in that most people (including, often, the writers themselves) fail to appreciate that the presence of female people is implied in these words. As a result, the participation of women in history and in political and social life is significantly obscured in English-speaking societies.

There are other ways in which the English language is used to discriminate against women. For example, the common habit of adding "lady" or "woman" as a qualifier to an occupation (a "woman lawyer") reinforces the idea that most occupations are properly all-male. Such phrases suggest that the person described is not a *true* professional. The use of a "feminine" suffix (a "sculptress" or a "majorette") also plays a large part in furthering the notion that in the real world of work achievement women are a kind of substandard variation on the male norm. The careful reader is likely to see that the introduction of such terms is usually gratuitous, the sex of the person concerned being irrelevant to the matter under discussion.

Many broadcasters and journalists describe women in terms of their marital status and physical appearance, whereas men would never be accorded similar treatment. For example, a British newspaper, the *Daily Express,* described a political event as follows: "Blonde bombshell Margaret Bain . . . took over as the glamorous face of Scottish Nationalism from party pin-up Margo Macdonald." Of course, this approach trivializes the actions and achievements of women in the public eye, and suggests that women's main function is to give pleasure to men. The same result is achieved through the common use of different words to describe similar feelings and activities on the part of men and women. For example, women "squabble" or "bicker," whereas men "argue" or "disagree." Women are "upset" or "emotional," whereas men are "concerned" or "angry."

When we come to the everyday words used for female human beings, the English language offers a particularly rich store of resonances and associations. "Girl" implies, among other things, immaturity and dependence; "lady" often connotes decorum and conformity; "woman" and "female" traditionally carry connotations of sexuality and reproduction. Although all these words can be used with respect and approbation, they are often employed as insults. Consider, for example, "he fights like a girl" or "he's an old woman" or "it's a womanish reaction." In this way, not only women but anything associated with them become objects for ridicule. It is interesting, but perhaps not surprising, to note that although it is almost always considered insulting to detect "feminine" traits in a man, the identification of "masculine" traits in a woman is usually considered to be a compliment. Many women are pleased to be told that "they think like a man," and "man-tailored" clothes are supposed to be "right" for the world of business. Even when a girl is referred to as a "tomboy," the epithet fails to carry the disapproval conveyed by the description of a boy as a "sissy."

Let us look a little more closely at two particularly ambiguous words: "lady" and "girl." I recall that on my first day as a copywriter/proofreader in the advertising department of a department store, I was solemnly informed by the department chief that "we never use 'ladies' here." I was instructed never to write, or allow to slip into the copy, the phrase "ladies' panties." The correct usage, apparently, was "women's undies." This incident helped me to understand for the first time that "lady" can, in different contexts, imply both respect and admiration and snobbish and trivializing condenscension. I refrain from exploring here the extraordinary convolutions of mind that transformed the despised "panties" into the apparently decorous "undies."

Outside an intimate relationship, few people would think of referring to a male person over the age of, say, eighteen as a "boy." Indeed, when this word was applied by white people to adult black men, it conveyed a clear message that a superior was addressing an inferior. Yet women commonly continue to be addressed as "girls" well into middle age. For many women, this comes more as an insult than the compliment it is perhaps intended to be. Applied to an adult woman, the word "girl" can be seen as patronizing and demeaning. Casey and Miller describe how, in response to such feelings among its staff, a major corporation launched a newspaper advertising campaign called "Let's get rid of 'The Girl.'" The most successful advertisement in the series ended with these remarks: "'The Girl' is certainly a woman when she's out of her teens. Like you, she has a name. Use it." The authors report that the campaign brought a huge response from readers, "including congratulatory telephone calls, telegrams, and even flowers."[7]

Minding One's Language

Some pundits have acknowledged the fact that the English language is biased in favor of the male but have gone on to express concern that any change in this area would lead to ugly linguistic distortions. They have also voiced fears that the language would become dull, bland, "unisex." Such arguments have been countered incisively by exponents of change. Far from wishing to encourage the development of a "unisex" language, they argue, they are fighting to see women made truly visible; they are in fact combating the *present* "unisex" tendency of English. Their concern is to sharpen language as a tool, not to blunt it. Thus, the sentence "men have always hoped to conquer disease" may more accurately be rephrased as, "the conquest of disease has always been the goal of human societies."

This last example was taken from Miller and Swift's *The Handbook of Non-Sexist Writing,* a manual intended for use by well-meaning but confused editors, writers, and speakers. Full of pertinent examples, the book shows how writing can avoid sexist bias and remain graceful and simple. One hopes that the message contained in this book, and in others like it, will percolate through the writing and publishing worlds.

There are signs of a growing realization that some of the old linguistic conventions are no longer appropriate for the societies involved. For example, in 1979 usage arbiters at the *New York Times* took a close look at its pages: "After three items had appeared in the same column of news briefs and mentioned, respectively, 'women students,' 'a woman photographer,' and 'a woman customer,' an in-house bulletin from the news desk commented: 'The use of *woman* as a modifier suggests that such words as *student, photographer,* and *customer,* unadorned, are masculine. . . . Probably the time has come to banish *woman* as an adjective; we don't use *man* that way. When a person's sex is truly newsworthy, let us use the same kinds of construction for both sexes: *male students, female students; lawyers who are women; lawyers who are men.'"[8]

Other newspapers and publishing houses also have developed guidelines on nonsexist language. In Britain, the national Union of Journalists, has produced a practical booklet entitled *Images of Women: Guidelines for Promoting Equality through Journalism.* Such guidelines encourage the use of English so that, where appropriate, women are given equal prominence with men. Writers are also advised on how to avoid the sex-role stereotyping so endemic in the culture and so damaging to the status of women.

In other fields, too, attempts are being made to adjust the lens of the language so that women come into focus as fully human beings. In religion, for example, hymns and prayers are being rewritten; in law, the wording of statutes is being revised to make clear the full citizenship of female human beings.

Surnames and Titles

"What's in a name?" is a question answered in many ways in the history and literature of cultures. People's names are inextricably bound up with their sense of identity and their reputation in the community; accordingly, they are assumed to have great psychological and social importance. A "good name" is equally important for a private individual, a politician, a professional person, and a retailer.

What, then, is the significance of the convention that, on marriage, a woman abandons her surname and assumes that of her husband? Traditionally, this change of name has been supposed to signify the beginning of a new life. From marriage onward, the woman is expected to devote herself primarily to the interests and well-being of her husband and children. No doubt, for a variety of reasons, many women have been happy to acquiesce to this change in their circumstances. Yet even in the nineteenth century, numbers of women objected to the loss of identity implicit in this change of name. For example, the American women's rights campaigner Lucy Stone refused (with her husband's complete agreement) to change her surname on marriage. Her example led to the formation in 1921 of the Lucy Stone League, the first organization to help women with the legal and bureaucratic difficulties involved in keeping their names after marriage.

At present, increasing numbers of women refuse to change their names on marriage. A decision of this kind may be made for a variety of reasons: a woman's reluctance to appear to be the property of her husband, her desire to express continuity in her life, or her wish to retain the "good name" she has made for herself in a professional or business capacity. When the decision is made solely for the last reason, women sometimes compromise by adopting their husband's name in private life and retaining their own name for professional purposes. This compromise sometimes works well but often causes considerable confusion — mainly as a result of the common journalistic habit of annexing a wife to her husband even when the marriage relation is in no way relevant to the event being reported. For example, *The Times* of London printed an article about a woman who had won an award for writing a children's book. The headline chosen: "Don's Wife's Award."

Women who decide not to change their names on marriage may face awesome social, administrative, and bureaucratic hurdles. Many are amazed to find outright hositlity to the notion that a woman should be free to use her own name. Such amazement is perhaps naive; after all, the convention is firmly rooted in a culture that consistently elevates the male sex above the female.

Over and above the personal significance of women changing their names, the convention has far-reaching cultural and historical implications. For example, it is very difficult for a woman (or a man) to trace maternal ancestors through public records. And many historians have noted that changes in name have greatly hampered detailed research into women's contribution to political and social movements.

Just as women change their name on marriage, so they are expected to change their title. During the late eighteenth century, the social title Miss (like Mrs., an abbreviation of the traditional title Mistress) began to be used to distinguish single women from married women. From that time on, a complex system of labeling developed that used changes of title and name to indicate whether a woman was single, married, divorced, or widowed. Men, meantime, continued to carry only the title of Mr., regardless of marital status.

Many women considered it unfair and unnecessary that their marital status became such a prominent part of their public persona, and the 1940s saw the introduction of the title Ms., which, like Mr., indicated gender only. Use of this title has now become widespread. Current social trends seem to indicate, in fact, that social titles of any kind are unnecessary.

Who Does the Talking?

Part of the feminine stereotype in many cultures is the supposed talkativeness of women. Given half a chance, it seems, women chatter away on trivial topics to anyone within earshot. Jokes and cartoons abound in which agonized husbands interpose a newspaper (real or metaphorical) between themselves and their relentlessly communicative wives.

Only recently, with the advent of feminist scholarship, has any substantial research been done on the relative talkativeness of men and women. And the findings show that, in both natural and artificial settings, men talk more than women. In addition, in mixed-sex conversations, men consistently interrupt women and take it upon themselves to define the topics for discussion. Dale Spender, a prominent researcher in this area, comments:

> It is relatively easy to substantiate the thesis that when women do not speak in terms that are acceptable to men, they do not get a proper hearing; in fact, it would sometimes be easy to substantitate that they get no hearing at all. Women are "queried," they are interrupted, their opinions are discounted and their contributions devalued in virtually all of the mixed-sex conversations that I have taped. And there is little doubt in my mind that females have traditionally reacted to this by retreating into silence.[9]

A "talkative" woman, it seems, does not speak nearly as much as a man who is *not* judged particularly loquacious. As in all areas of life, the standards by which women are judged are not the same as those used for men.

Naturally enough, many women respond to the difficulties they find in communicating with men by preferring to talk to other women. In women-only conversations, it seems that speaking and listening roles are more equally divided and that speakers are much less likely to compete for attention. Dale Spender reports the words of one of her female interviewees:

> There are so many things you have to be conscious of when you talk to men. And they are not there when you talk to the girls. I don't have to flatter any of my (women) friends, for example. It's much more sincere. I don't keep thinking, Will they think me silly? When I'm talking to my (women) friends I don't keep asking myself what they want to hear, and then try and say it. I don't really ask what will make them feel good and then say it . . . but I don't say things that upset them, it's not that. It just doesn't arise. I just talk. I'm sure we all do. I think it's just easier.[10]

The contemporary women's movement early recognized the importance of women being allowed to define their reality through discussion and talk; for this reason, they excluded men from their "consciousness-raising groups."

In these groups women talked, listened, and shared their experiences, exploring together how their personal, political, and work lives had been shaped by a male-dominated society. A fresh look was taken at what might be considered "trivial" or "important"; and new insights, which continue to inform feminist critiques of society, were developed into the relationship between the "personal" and the "political." In refusing to accept men's criteria for "proper" discussion and conversation, these women came to find a different way of approaching the world.

Although many women now actively oppose the ways in which common patterns of communication and language relegate them to second place, many other women are struggling to gain a footing in the public world where the rules for success in communication are entirely man-made. The last decade has seen a plethora of manuals for ambitious women. These manuals advise the selection of a well-tailored suit for business wear and give pointers on how to increase assertiveness, project a female voice, and communicate talent and sincerity. Readers of such manuals are busily learning a second language in order to communicate more effectively with men, who need only the language they grew up with.

There is a further catch. Women must also make sure, the experts say, never to put their femininity in doubt. The difficulty of such an enterprise can be seen in the results of studies of student perceptions of women faculty in American universities. Even when male professors communicate in traditionally authoritative fashion and are known to be less expert in their subject matters, students have been found to prefer male to female faculty. It seems that the female professors either do not meet their expectations of how professors should talk or do not conform to their idea of what women should be like. A true "damned if you do and damned if you don't" situation.[11]

Many people believe that if considerable numbers of women were to get a foothold in public life, accepted styles of communication and debate would change for the better. The 300 Group (dedicated to getting more women into the British Parliament) has suggested that their presence would change the very character of the House of Commons. The group's Information Officer has been quoted as saying, "There may well be more cross-floor consultation, a more reasonable atmosphere, much less of the sort of bear-baiting men seem to enjoy." The newspaper columnist who gave space to this representative went on to comment:

> Public debate, in or out of the House, is frequently made rigid and uncreative by the rules of male protocol that confine men themselves. I cannot count the number of times that I, myself,

have sat in a lather of fright, listening to men carefully avoiding what seem to be central issues, the "whys," and in the end stammered out my thoughts, to be met with a sigh of relief all round, partly because the men, too, wanted that subject discussed and partly because they obviously felt that a woman could better afford to look a fool. Even untrained we can play an important role. Trained, who knows what we may achieve?[12]

Women and Children's Literatue

Nursery rhymes and fairy tales provide children of both sexes with the opportunity to be baffled, excited, disturbed, and soothed. Their strong feelings of love, hate, envy, and jealousy are brought to bear on situations and characters exotically removed from the family circle. A combination of familiar and unfamiliar words and situations stimulates in the child's imagination intensely vivid images and associations.

For girl children, however, the associations provoked by nursery rhymes and fairy tales may presage later lessons that women are less active, less capable, and less adventurous than men. Fairy tales such as that of Sleeping Beauty also transmit the message that the high point of any girl's life will be her rescue (from boredom or danger) by an eminently eligible young man.

Fairy tales and nursery rhymes often began as allegorical tales, or fables. Sometimes they were based on political events and served as a safe vehicle for gossip. These tales that remained part of folk tradition and survived many changes in political ideologies have some core of moral preachment to communicate. For example, Humpty Dumpty's great fall carries with it the message that breaking things is bad and that once broken, things cannot be mended no matter how hard you try.

Fairy tales were (and are) told to children by nursemaids and mothers. A goose is a protective but silly creature who will not only swallow whatever she happens past but will incorporate it into her being to her own eventual destruction. Like this silly, self-destructive, but nurturant creature named Mother Goose, women carry forward the symbols of the group past. Where is Father Gander? Nowhere to be found. The closest mythical father involved in communicating cultural values to new generations is Santa Claus (Father Christmas in England). He rewards and punishes behavior; knows everything; and silently, secretly, and without direct contact provides material benefits and wish fulfillments for little children.

Nursery rhymes provide cultural messages on many levels at once. Besides the obvious moral to these little stories, they vividly portray differential and deferential behaviors for boys and girls. Let's just compare two fairly commonplace and similar rhymes: Little Miss Muffett and Little Jack Horner. Both of them are quietly and happily eating away at pleasant foods, but when you learn what happens to each of them, you learn a big difference between little boys and little girls and what they can expect from the world.

Little Jack Horner	Little Miss Muffet
Sat in a corner	Sat on a tuffet
Eating his Christmas pie	Eating her curds and whey
He put in a thumb	Along came a spider
And pulled out a plum	Who sat down beside her
Saying, *"What a good boy am I."*	And *frightened Miss Muffet away.*

Jack Horner did something quite naughty, really. He put his thumb into the pie. But he was rewarded for his misbehavior. He got a plum, and recognizing his reward, he happily declared his state of grace. Miss Muffet did nothing either naughty or good, but presumably eating nourishing ordinary fare is rewarded by the encroachment of a spider, which evoked the traditional female response to such creatures — fear. She ran away from her food in the end. Thus, little boys may be rewarded even for infractions of good table manners, whereas little girls respond to events totally outside their control by running away.

When a boy and girl are mentioned together, we again get a message of difference and deference.

> Jack and Jill went up a hill
> To fetch a pail of water.
> Jack fell down and broke his crown
> And Jill came tumbling after.

Why must Jill fall down after Jack does? Is she unable to maintain her own balance if unaccompanied by her brother? Must she always follow and never lead? We get the message about which sex sets the tone for the society.

Other rhymes are free of sex-role distinctions, but carry messages about appropriate role behaviors. For instance:

> Mary, Mary, quite contrary
> How does your garden grow?
> With silver bells and cockle shells
> And pretty maids, all in a row.

Early school readers are likely to reinforce such images. Boys *do*, while girls *are*. Fathers go off to work at interesting and important jobs, which are often made more interesting by the addition of a uniform or a fine-sounding title. Women are on the whole confined to the unglamorous domestic barracks. They bake, clean, dress and direct children, call people to dinner, and along with little girls, get into terrible messes from which they must be rescued by men and boys. In these basic readers, girls watch, weep, and often fall victim to the pranks of mischievous boys. Such readers discourage girls from thinking of themselves as active, capable people; they also fail to provide boys with any models of behavior that are not stereotypically masculine.

On those rare occasions when outstanding women are described in a history text, they are explained away in phrases like "Amelia Earhart from the beginning was not like other little girls. . . ." In picture after picture, girls are spectators. They look on, they admire, they are recipients — but rarely are they initiators. Characteristically, these little girls embody the fairy tale of Sleeping Beauty. They are Jills who tumble down after Jacks. The women who take control and make determinations in school readers and fairy tales are old, ugly witches. They have power.

Even female royalty is portrayed poorly in these books. The princess lacks power, control, or even self-determination. She is "beautiful and good," but the king "commands, orders, leads." The classic textbook picture of Queen Victoria shows her as a young girl in night clothes being informed that her uncle has died and she will be crowned. Her masculine predecessors are generally portrayed in such manly tasks as reviewing the guard or leading a battle.

It is almost impossible to find in a school text the description of a famous man as a husband and father. The reverse is true for women. Marie Curie's predicament as wife and mother is mentioned as prominently as her scientific genius. And while children's literature is replete with examples of wailing females, it is extraordinary to find a man or boy engaged in tenderness, crying, or weakness. Men simply are not allowed the scope in emotional expression that women are permitted; at the same time, women are not admitted into the assembly of the strong.

One children's book editor commented to me that "the change to nonsexist writing is not substantial, but it is significant. Most traditional children's writers are women, but they tend to be conservative and not much interested in feminism. They think that sex-role stereotyping doesn't really matter — it'll all come out in the wash. But the major publishers and newer authors are beginning to think differently — and that changed attitude can be seen in a fair proportion of the books now being published."

Literary Looks at Women

Some of the earliest arguments presented by the women's movement in the 1960s were aimed at the representation of women in the media and through popular literature. But two hundred years earlier, the English novel *Pamela* brought together the main philosophical/literary traditions on women: the ideas of Christian and courtly (romantic) love. These ideas shared the view of woman as virginal-pure (the good-mother image along with virginal purity) and the image of woman as evil, sensuous, and destructive.

It is neither surprising nor perverse that literary views of women are essentially mirrors of men. They are literary devices through which the conflicts, strivings, achievements, and maturation process of a man's psyche, as well as his social class, political status, and cultural origins, may be illuminated. Even when *Pamela, Moll Flanders, Fanny Hill,* and *Emma* ostensibly provided a woman's-eye view of life, they actually presented women as victims of men's complex and clever manipulations. Women's problems were focused on courtship or on resolving the problem of accepting their place in the private sphere.

In any case, the female characterization served the novelist as the personification of emotional reactions to the (male) heroes' actions. Sexuality itself was presented from a masculine perspective and was female only in the uses made of it by the Dark Woman — the sensuous and destructive woman — who stood for base depravity as only a woman could embody it. Women could be this unidimensional if they were not rational, intellectual, or dynamic beings. And indeed, novelists of the eighteenth, nineteenth, and even twentieth centuries have seldom strayed from this overworked image.

Many of the best-known American novelists of the nineteenth century simply avoided having woman characters in their novels. *Moby Dick, Huckleberry Finn, The Last of the Mohicans,* and *The Red Badge of Courage* include women only occasionally, and then as abstract and vaporous beings who flit symbolically through the story to represent an idea with which the male hero grapples. Some notable exceptions to these popular portrayals include the works o˙ Mary Wollstonecraft and the French feminists of the eighteenth and nineteenth centuries. (What is particularly striking in this recital is that many of the novelists who presented this biased view of women were women.) Charles Brockden Brown, an American novelist strongly influenced by Mary Wollstonecraft, attempted in his novels to present rational, self-directed women and arguments for the education and emancipation of women. His books presage the arrival of the New Woman in literature.

There were contrasts among women writers in the nineteenth century in their presentations of women. Although writing was often the only creative art open to women, expectations and conventions usually resulted in novels of "manners," such as those of Jane Austen. Austen focused on women in her novels, but the characters were sentimentalists, in the tradition of the period. Their sphere was domestic; their emotions ran from love to suffering (but never to sexual passion even if the woman experienced sexuality) to sympathy but never to outraged anger; and they were ambitious only in terms of achieving a good marriage.

The novels of the Brontë sisters were remarkable in their portrayal of women as complete persons. Charlotte Brontë's *Jane Eyre* typified a Brontë heroine: she was capable, rational, intelligent, and independent; and she did not see marriage as her primary objective. In most Brontë heroines there is a reflection of an acute awareness of and paintful confrontation with sex-role restrictions. As writers, the Brontës adopted masculine pen names; they recognized the near impossibility of being seriously received by editors or the reading public as women. Adopting male pseudonyms was also the course taken by George Elliot and George Sand.

Some men of letters in the nineteenth century recognized the conventional woman presented in literature as a symbol of the generally bourgeois and materialistic morality of the times. As a reaction against the system, they created literary and theatrical masterpieces that are relevant to people and events a century after their creation. George Bernard Shaw, Henrik Ibsen, James Joyce, and Henry James depicted women facing and resolving dilemmas imposed by social stereotypes and their own upbringing. Yet these authors, although able to depict female protagonists as complete human beings, were unable to imagine a *happy* resolution to their dilemmas.

The Woman as Earth Mother, who reveled in her femininity and combined the virtuous with the sensuous — like Mollie Bloom in Joyce's *Ulysses* — affirmed life in the revolt against bourgeois morality, but this did not take her out of the bedroom either. And women who abandoned their traditional role were doomed to madness and death.

Again we are reminded that men who defy conventions are not diminished through their personal lives or confined to the status imposed by their marital condition. Women who do likewise, in fact or fiction, end tragically.

The Great Tradition?

In literature, as in many other academic fields, feminist critics and scholars have pointed out that women's contribution to the subject has been downplayed. Also, they argue, many influential and highly regarded authors have won their acclaim largely through their skilled and vivid representations of men's mastery over women. In her pioneering work *Sexual Politics,* Kate Millett has incisively and wittily dissected works by D.H. Lawrence, Henry Miller, and Norman Mailer, uncovering misogyny that underlies, and contributes to, the glorification of their heroes.[13]

Contemporary feminists have begun to show that women have a literary tradition of their own that, like women themselves, has been largely ignored. The nineteenth century, for example, saw a positive explosion of talented and successful women novelists, many of whom, like Kate Chopin, were virtually forgotten until feminist publishers reprinted their work. In the twentieth century, innovative and important writers like Sylvia Townsend Warner and Christina Stead have been supplanted in popular esteem and university syllabi by male writers of notably less talent and stature. The distinguished American poet Adrienne Rich has commented on this phenomenon:

> The entire history of women's struggle for self-determination has been muffled in silence over and over. One serious cultural obstacle encountered by any feminist writer is that each feminist work has tended to be received as if it emerged from nowhere: as if each of us had lived, thought and worked without any historical past or contextual present. This is one of the ways in which women's work and thinking has been made to seem sporadic, erratic, orphaned of any tradition of its own.[14]

Social attitudes and conventions imposed limitations and constraints on both the lives and work of women writers. When, for example, the as yet unpublished Charlotte Brontë asked advice from Robert Southey, a well-known poet, he replied in the following terms:

> The day dreams in which you habitually indulge are likely to induce a distempered state of mind; and, in proportion as all the ordinary uses of the world seem to you flat and unprofitable, you will be unfitted for them without becoming fitted for anything else. Literature cannot be the business of a woman's life and it ought not to be. The more she is engaged in her proper duties, the less leisure she will have for it, even as an accomplishment and a reaction. . . .[15]

Many years later, Virginia Woolf described how, before she could take herself and her writing seriously, she had to do battle with a certain phantom she christened "The Angel of the House" after a famous Victorian poem extolling the virtues of the wife and mother. She described the phantom as "intensely sympathetic. She was immensely charming. She was utterly unselfish. She excelled in the difficult arts of family life. She sacrificed herself daily. If there was chicken, she took the leg; if there was a draught she sat in it — in short she was so constituted that she never had a mind or a wish of her own, but preferred to sympathize always with the minds and wishes of others. Above all — I need not say it — she was pure." The advice given to the young writer by this kindly phantom included the admonition to "be sympathetic; be tender; flatter; deceive." Woolf goes on to relate that she seized this phantom in a murderous grasp, giving as her reason: "Had I not killed her she would have killed me."[16]

Pressures for women's conformity in subject matter and style have continued. In the early 1970s, for example, the Canadian writer Jane Rule published a novel that included a sensitive depiction of a lesbian love affair. Critics had different responses. One called the book "intelligent, well-bred, skillful, sensitive and always in good taste." But then added: "It never breaks through into the roughness and mystery of fully rounded life." Another wrote: "There's more hairy-chested hormones in this one book than the first six from the pen of Truman Capote, but it's all coursing through ostensibly female veins."

In literature as in life, women are supposed to be silent on matters disturbing to men; and if they speak (or write) they are expected to do so in a muted voice. The lasting irony is that the muted voice is then criticized as too feeble and timid to achieve excellence.

It is one of the triumphs of the contemporary women's movement that this situation is slowly changing. Feminist publishers and printers are now carrying out the work of rehabilitating forgotten writers of worth and encouraging and publishing new women writers. Their efforts have been so successful that many mainstream publishers have recognized the value of women's writing and a "women's market" and have adapted their lists accordingly. It is becoming increasingly difficult for even the most conservative male reviewer to scribble the offhand but value-laden dismissal, "a woman's novel."

The current "pocket romances," authored for the most part by women, although sometimes by men who have assumed feminine pen names, are curious descendants of the nineteenth-century's idea of women's reading matter. Their popularity depends on their marketing, which is largely managed in supermarkets and drugstores, places where women are likely to be consumers. The "romances" are inexpensive and are oriented to a lower than average reading level. Market research on book buying reveals most book buyers are women; nevertheless, sales of these "romances" indicate that they are also being purchased by men! Mass literary tastes may have become androgynized, and in order to become a best seller, a book may soon have to appeal to women and men.

Notes

1. Jerome Kagan, "Acquisition and Significance of Sex Typing and Sex Role Identity," in *Review of Child Development Research,* ed. M. J. Hoffman and L. W. Hoffman Vol. 1 (New York: Russell Sage Foundation, 1964).
2. Personal communication with talmudic scholar Rabbi I. Reich, 1980.
3. Elizabeth Gould Davis, *The First Sex* (New York: Viking Penguin, 1972).
4. Casey Miller and Kate Swift, *The Handbook of Non-Sexist Writing* (New York: Lippincott 1980).
5. Ibid.
6. Ibid.
7. Ibid.
8. Ibid.
9. Robin Lakoff, *Language and Woman's Place* (New York: Harper & Row, 1975).
10. Ibid.
11. Ibid.
12. Miller and Swift, *Handbook of Non-Sexist Writing.*
13. Kate Millett, *Sexual Politics,* (Garden City, N.Y.: Doubleday, 1969).
14. Adrienne Rich, *Of Woman Born,* (New York: Norton, 1976).
15. Cynthis Griffin Wolf, "A Mirror for Men: Stereotypes of Women in Literature," in *Woman: An Issue,* ed. Lee R. Edwards, Mary Heath, and Lisa Baskin (Boston: Little, Brown, 1972).

Chapter 5 FEMALE SEXUALITY

The sexuality of women has been surrounded with more publicity — and more ignorance — than almost any other area of human life. This discussion starts, not with yet another exploration of the female reproductive system, but with the sexual gratification of women. It starts where most discussions of *male* sexuality begin.

Until recently, nearly all information — and misinformation — about women's sexuality came from men. A century ago, an eminent British doctor, Sir William Acton, wrote: "The majority of women (happily for society) are not troubled with sexual feelings of any kind."[1] In common with many others of his time, he truly believed that the "normal woman" found her greatest physical and emotional satisfaction in bearing and rearing children and making her husband's life comfortable, and that an active sexual interest on her part constituted an abnormality or even a disease. Later sexologists disputed this view — the view of a man who, it may be noted, held that "virility" in men was much more highly developed than "maternity" in women. (To a modern woman virility and maternity are hardly equivalents; maternity describes womanhood even less accurately than virility describes manhood.)

From Sigmund Freud to Havelock Ellis, definitions, descriptions, and explanations of women's sexual nature were presented in terms of women's response to, or imitation of, male sexuality. Female "frigidity," a Freudian notion revived by the "sexual radicals" of the 1950s, denoted not neurosis but a woman's failure to respond to a male partner in the manner demanded.

More recent studies — in particular the work of Masters and Johnson and that of Hite — revealed what many women and men must have known but not admitted: women's sexuality is much more active, and more complicated, than had hitherto been accepted. Shere Hite conducted a nationwide survey of female sexuality by distributing detailed questionnaires to a large sample of women of all ages and in all walks of life. Her findings indicated overwhelmingly that the things that give a woman sexual pleasure are not, by and large, those expected in, and anxiously promoted by, a penis-centered culture. The penis was of minor importance compared to its possessor's ability to understand and respond to a women's pattern of sexual

67

arousal. Indeed, on a physical level, many women found masturbation far more gratifying than traditional heterosexual intercourse. Many women valued sex as much for the physical intimacy and emotional closeness it brings as for the genital excitement it arouses. And women's definitions of sexual feelings tended to be much broader than those offered by men.

What, then, has been discovered about this active and complicated female sexual response? Most important, women have an organ, the clitoris, that has only one purpose: the transmission of sexual pleasure. There is no comparable male organ. Formerly, the clitoris was presumed to be a vestigial penis and to respond to stimulation as a penis does, by enlarging and erecting. Since scientists (predominantly male) were at a loss to appreciate or understand female sexuality, this was the presumption that prevailed. But clitoral stimulation and orgasm have recently been more closely studied, to give a more accurate picture of sexual arousal. When sexual tension is at its highest, the clitoris fills with blood and swells, and the glans or tip of the organ retracts under its hood. Orgasm may result from direct stimulation of the clitoris or may be the climax of sensations transmitted to the clitoris from the vagina and other regions of the body.[2]

Women differ in the length of time they take to reach orgasm. Kinsey and his associates, in their survey of more than 8000 women, found that those who reached orgasm during intercourse (fewer than 50 percent of the sample) did so after an average of five minutes; but 12 percent of his sample took ten minutes or more.[3] There is also considerable evidence to suggest that all women are not only potentially orgasmic but are potentially multiorgasmic. That is, after reaching an initial climax, they can, with additional stimulation, achieve a succession of climaxes. The vast majority of men lack the capacity to go from one orgasm to another without a period of respite and new stimulation. Another fact of female sexuality is that, with the exception of the very sensitive glans of the clitoris, the areas capable of greatest sexual sensation differ from one woman to another and from one act of intercourse to another.

Contrary to popular male belief, the vagina, except for the outermost third, is the least sensitive part of a woman's sexual equipment. Thrusting and rubbing the penis against the walls of the vagina is not necessarily stimulating; indeed, it can blur sensation and even cause pain. A woman's sexual sensations and gratification are a function of her participation and activity. That is why positions of intercourse that confine or prohibit movement for the woman are likely to frustrate gratification. Active contractions of the vagina during intercourse do more than tone up the muscles used in childbirth; they contribute to orgasm.

Women's sexual behavior and their attitudes toward sexuality depend largely on prevailing social attitudes and behavior. As we moved from a traditionally repressive sexual climate into the "permissive" air of the 1960s women were faced with a whole new set of pressures. Orgasms — or at least decent fakes — became obligatory to satisfy the pleasure-insistent partner. Manuals of sexual techniques reinforced the message that sex was good but more sex (and with more men) was even better. The same comments applied in reverse, though with far less force, to men.

What women actually wanted from sex, physically and emotionally, was a question that remained largely unasked until the women's movement gained momentum in the 1970s. Today women are beginning to recognize the validity of their private, individual feelings about sex, and they are rejecting two basic assumptions: (1) that the purpose of female sexuality is male pleasure, and (2) that there is a blueprint or an ideal for female sexuality.

A clear example of women's reassessment of their sexuality is the increased acceptability of lesbian releationships. Once regarded as bizarre, intense physical and emotional relationships between women are now recognized as valid alternatives to heterosexual relationships. Many feminists acknowledge such relationships as offering more in the way of emotional closeness and physical harmony than sexual relationships between women and men.

The Control of Fertility

Clearly women's feelings about their sexuality are substantially influenced by whether they are able to control their fertility. This in turn depends on legal, medical, and social controls and on the attitudes of male partners.

Contraception, considered at times immoral, unnatural, and socially dangerous, is something that most women in the Western world now regard as a right. They also regard it as socially responsible, financially sensible, and contributing to their autonomy as individuals. Globally speaking, we have reached a point where birth control is not only optional but essential. The world's population continues to grow at an alarming rate. With this overpopulation come appalling poverty, overcrowding, crime, social and political unrest, pollution, and the destruction of irreplaceable natural resources. But political solutions and individual freedom of choice do not always go together. Sterilization programs in the Third World, for example, commonly fail to take account of the wishes of individual women and men.

The three essential components of effective action to limit population growth are political will, with solid "grass roots" backing; the wide availability of a range of contraceptive techniques; and the creation of socioeconomic and health conditions that will make high birthrates unnecessary.

The most commonly used methods of contraception are coitus interruptus, or the withdrawal of the penis from the vagina just before ejaculation; mechanical interference, where a device is inserted into the vagina to cover the cervix or put over the penis to prevent sperm from reaching the uterus; chemical interference, where spermicidal preparations are introduced into the vagina either before or after intercourse; abstinence or the "rhythm method," which involves calculating the fertile days in a woman's monthly cycle and abstaining from intercourse on those days; implanting long-term devices (IUDs) in the uterus, which prevents fertilized eggs from embedding themselves in the walls of the uterus; oral contraceptives, or "the Pill" in its various forms, which operate hormonally to create a condition of pseudo pregnancy in which ovulation ceases; and surgical interference, including tubal ligation or, in the case of men, vasectomy.

With any method there are physical and psychological costs, but these costs are evaluated as less than the cost of unwanted pregnancy. Withdrawal is unsatisfying for both partners and can disrupt the sexual response; caps and condoms can destroy the spontaneity of lovemaking; spermicides are less reliable than oral contraceptives; the Pill is not suitable for long-term use; IUDs can get disloged; abstinence at certain times of the month is probably the least reliable method because ovulation does not necessarily occur at the midpoint of every woman's cycle, and the cycle itself is easily upset; and although surgical sterilization does not affect sexual performance or gratification, it is generally irreversible.

Almost always, it is the woman who takes contraceptive precautions, often without consulting her partner. The risks outlined above are also hers. In other words, most women tacitly accept responsibility for their sexual activities. Until men accept similar responsibilities, women cannot fairly be blamed for regarding birth-control decisions as a "right." Ironically, the prejudice that men are not responsible for their sexual activities in the same way that woman are is partly maintained by women. The very small scale of research into contraceptives for men is to some extent a reflection of this prejudice.

But if women believe that contraception is ultimately their responsibility, might it not be legitimate to ask that they deliberately and collectively shoulder the responsibility for "saving the world" from lethal overpopulation? Overall, if one looks at the growing body of research on women's attitudes toward fertility and contraception, one finds that women want to control the number of pregnancies they have; they want to provide a better quality of life for fewer children. Where women have taken control of their fertility, living standards have risen. Where women are active participants in the economic, political, and social life of their communities, the birthrate has fallen. Is it the present and future role of women to stabilize the planet's population?

Contraception prevents the union of egg and sperm; induced abortion (as opposed to spontaneous abortion, or miscarriage) denies life to the product of such a union, to the fetus. Induced abortion remains a subject of passionate controversy. Some women, as well as some men, see it as violating the rights of the fetus. Others, mostly women, see the choice to abort or not as representative of a woman's right to control her own body, as an ultimate and inalienable human right.

Contrary to popular myth, abortion "on demand" has not led the majority of pregnant single women and teenagers to seek it. In fact, younger teenagers, when they learn that they are pregnant, tend to want to have the baby. In the United States and Western Europe the single parent is an increasingly common phenomenon. No one bothers to ask whether the mother was married at the time the child was conceived (fathers, of course, never were asked the same question). Most women seeking abortions today have pressing economic, health, or psychological reasons for doing so, over and above the fact of not being married.[4]

In some cultures abortion is used as a means of contraception. But while research into the psychological and physical aftermath of abortion suggests that there are seldom adverse consequences to a legally procured abortion and that abortion often poses fewer physical hazards than carrying a pregnancy to term, it is also very clear that repeated abortion is not a satisfactory means of birth control. Indeed, it may be physically dangerous.

Almost as many ethical questions surround the new field of reproductive engineering, which covers techniques of artifical insemination (for infertile couples and lesbian couples); fertilization outside the womb (to produce so-called test-tube babies); gestation *in vitro* and in artificial wombs; surrogate mothering (where the biological mother is infertile or unable to carry a pregnancy to term); and, soon, the manipulation of the genetic contents of egg and sperm so that human beings can be bred to desirable specifications.[5] Though some feminists see reproductive engineering as yet another arena in which male expertise will be used to subordinate women, most see it as science in the service of reproductive choice.

Childbirth

A woman's feelings about her sexuality are inevitably linked to society's treatment of pregnancy and childbirth. If sexual intercourse leads, nine months later, to increased poverty and extreme physical and emotional hardship, then the "joy of sex," if present in the first place, is likely to evaporate quickly. The following acount comes from a collection of letters written in 1915 by British working-class mothers:

> When my third baby arrived, I regret to say it was disfigured with a harelip, from which cause it could not take its food properly which caused it to cry almost incessantly, and after a trying period of eleven weeks, she, poor little mite, succumbed. Owing to the worry connected to this misfortune, and for want of rest, I felt my health giving way, and being in a weak condition, I became an easy prey for sexual intercourse, and thus once more I became a mother in fourteen months.[6]

Until recently, most societies have seen childbirth and postnatal care as women's processes. Parturition is an essential part of the bond between women and involves a great deal of mutual support. In Western societies in earlier centuries, men had little or nothing to do with childbirth; those in attendance were female midwives, many of whom had borne children themselves. But as the medical profession grew in power and status, women's reproductive function was seen as a profitable new area for specialization, and gynecology and obstetrics emerged as professional male preserves. Over a number of years, culminating only during the present century, female midwives were discredited and demoted in status.

One result of this social change is that childbirth has become a clinical procedure in which the role of the mother is generally subordinate to the practices of the hospital and the overwhelmingly male medical profession. Although the working-class mother quoted above may well have welcomed the medical care now given to pregnant and post-parturant women, many women today resent the dehumanization and institutionalization of childbirth. Other women note, with a cynical eye, that the doctrine of "childbirth without fear" is handed on to them primarily by male human beings in no risk of undergoing the experience themselves. And some have observed, no less wryly, that childbirth happens to have been labeled a "marvelous experience" at precisely the time in Western history when women have more choice in the matter than ever before. Now that having children is not the inevitable lot of women, perhaps the product has to be newly packaged and promoted to be tempting.

Women as Sex Objects

A woman's view of her sexuality also depends on how her sex as a whole is regarded by men — by individual men and by male attitudes current in the larger cultural and social spheres.

Anatomy dictates that men can force sexual intercourse on women, whereas women cannot "rape" men. Not infrequently, this fact has been used to justify as somehow "natural" the rape of women by men. Rape is not a titillating corollary to consensual sex; it is not even more-than-ordinarily-violent sexual intercourse suffused with the added excitement of the chase. Women who fantasize rape, and a number of women find such fantasies sexually arousing, are not fantasizing about the real thing. They are making a fantasy out of Western society's glorification of the male sex drive. Rape is not related to any romantic urge but to the fear and contempt that, at the deepest level of their being, many men feel toward women. The aim of the rapist is not to take pleasure (indeed, can pleasure be "taken" from another human being?) but to inflict degradation and humiliation. (That is the spirit in which rioting male prisoners anally rape captured prison guards.) Few men, reassured since birth that they are the hunters in the sexual jungle, see the ugly truth behind rape. [7]

One of the most bitter cruelties associated with Western society's worship of masculinity and the male sex drive ("a man's gotta do what a man's gotta do") is that women have been subjected to the belief that their natural sexuality is passive, even masochistic. In a very real sense women have been reared as rape victims — as unable and even unwilling to deny men their "natural rights."

Fortunately, ideology of this kind is on the wane, but it retains some residual force in the still popular assumption that women who have been raped must have been "asking for it." In cases where the "asking for it" philosophy has held sway, it is often discovered that the woman in question was merely exercising her freedom to act and behave without excessive caution — as any boy or man would do, unthinkingly. It was in retaliation to the idea that to be safe women must forego certain personal freedoms (e.g., the freedom to walk in a city at night) that women's groups in Britain organized demonstrations under the banner "Reclaim the night."

The women's movement has set up rape crisis centers, staffed by women who offer support and help to rape victims. Many rape victims, with

reason, are afraid of being subjected to the insulting and degrading treatment meted out by the police and the courts.

In pornography the degradation of women is implicit and explicit. The
traditional question asked about pornography (literally, "the graphic depiction of whores") is whether the frequently violent nature of the material
leads to violence against women. One contemporary feminist writer, Andrea
Dworkin, maintains that this question evades the reality of the situation.
She argues that pornography is itself violence against women – and very
profitable violence. The pornography industry in the United States is larger
than the record and film industries put together. Other writers argue that
pornography exacerbates the contempt in which women are generally held
in Western society. Pornography, it is claimed, is the baseline for men's
view of women.[8]

The literary sexual revolution has as its epitome the *Playboy* magazine
empire. Norman Mailer was at the height of his notoriety (and Henry
Miller's work, illegally imported into the United States, was widely cir-
culated) when Hugh Hefner brought out the first issue of *Playboy*, in which
the sexually liberated woman became a "bunny" to be a plaything for
Playboys. Una Stannard, writing in 1968, analyzed the *Playboy* phenomenon as follows:

> The club's bunny symbol is so visible because the boys
> themselves, like the rabbit that led Alice down the hole to
> Wonderland, have a tendency to vanish. They tend to become
> invisible because they are almost always playing their favorite
> game: a unique version of "doctor," a spectator sport for boys
> which involves lurking behind the scenes and examining girls in
> the all-together spread-eagled or folded up in various
> positions.[9]

The success of *Playboy* led not only to the extension of a bunny-marked
empire in leisure pursuits and hedonistic ambitions but also to the prolifera-
tion of the idea in magazines such as *Oui, Penthouse, Hustler,* and *Screw.*
The objective of pornography is to arouse the reader by portraying sexual
relations in which all the conventional standards are violated and the only
psychological feelings involved are lust and the relief of sexual tensions.

The consequences of the legitimation of pornography given by the sexual
revolution is further alienation between men and women in everyday relationships as well as a pernicious effect on sexual intercourse and mature sexual fulfillment. Whenever a social philosophy extols or glorifies the object

characteristics of a person, it deprives the individual or group of integrity. In brief, such productions arouse impossible expectations by some people of others and by others of themselves.

Pornography is contrary to the idea of literary productions as a kind of transcendent fantasy or a transcendent criticism. The language grammar itself dictates that a person is a subject. As a dynamic active quantity in the equation of an art production, the person cannot be recipient/reaction and be believable, real, ideal, or honest.

In prostitution, as in rape and pornography, women have been assigned the role of passive object, ripe for exploitation and degradation. All three phenomena are deeply related to women's subordinate place in society and to men's view of their sexuality and worth. In Bangladesh, for example, it is a matter of strict social custom that a virgin who has been raped should take to prostitution.

The age-old assumption — in most societies, not merely in the West — that men have abundant and varied sexual needs that must not be denied has inevitably resulted in the creation of a class of professionally unchaste women who provide sexual services for men. This double standard permeates the whole phenomenon of prostitution.

The 1956 British Sexual Offenses Act, for example, was restricted to women (although a more recent piece of legislation, the Street Offenses Bill, removed legal distinctions between men and women). Customers and pimps are much less frequently confronted with the legal code than are prostitutes. Less than a decade ago, many states in America upheld laws that enacted different penalties for prostitutes and their clients. In New Jersey, for instance, for the same offenses men were given a specific sentence; women were given indeterminate sentences that resulted in longer imprisonment. Similarly, considerable social stigma has always been attached to the prostitute, whereas little or no stigma attaches to her client.[10]

Most prostitutes are women. Of those men who do become prostitutes, it is interesting to note the similarities between them and their female counterparts. First, their clients are nearly all male. Second, male prostitutes are usually poor, unskilled, and on the margins of society. Female prostitution is, and always has been, the product of economic deprivation and sexual double standards.

The Future and the Past

The twentieth century has witnessed considerable changes in expectations, knowledge, and the experience of sexuality by women. We might delude ourselves into believing that these changes, once established, will augur well for future generations. We might also believe that some of the conflicts women now experience about their sexuality will be resolved in favor of more and better. It is worthwhile, then, to look back to see if anyone else has ever been in this "progressive" predicament and to learn what may follow from it.

Female sexuality was an accepted fact of life among pre-Christian Gaelic Celts, whose Brehon law provided maximally for the enjoyment of a variety of partners and relationships by women as well as men. It would also seem that ancient Jewish society provided for the expectation of women's sexual gratification by both biblical and talmudic laws that required a husband to have sexual intercourse with his wife at a prescribed level of frequency depending upon his occupation. Further codicils and admonitions assured that men would be sexually considerate and humane not only with their wives but with all women.

Let us consider a few of the social and psychological factors that contributed to the annihilation of these sexual codes. For the ancient Irish society, contrary to the suggestions of many scholars, the introduction of Christianity did little to change sexual behaviors. If anything, there was added concern for women's well-being and potential with the elimination of their military service and alternative arrangements that required the consent of a consort before a man could dispose of property and inheritance rights. The change in women's control of their sexuality resulted from the imposition of English common law and primogeniture on the society.

Jewish women, after generations of survival struggles, became the focus for procreation. Their role as breeders and feeders was emphasized with each succeeding threat to survival, either as a religious entity or as human beings. Assimilation and extermination produced the Jewish Mother image to the exclusion of the sexual woman.

English common law descended from the ancient system Solon imposed on Greek society. Societies under threat and men and women under siege do not promote the most humane and progresssive brands of knowledge. To use terminology from psychology, these two exemplary groups suffered aversive conditioning in relearning sexuality. Wars and violence forced women into breeder and feeder roles and dehumanized them entirely through their sexuality.

The twenty-first century will begin with more knowledge and understanding of human sexuality among a wider proportion of the earth's population than ever before. In the twentieth century women in many countries provided support and protection for each other's sexuality by banding together to create rape crisis centers and shelters for battered wives, to change rape and incest laws, and to teach each other to understand their bodies and make their own choices on pregnancy. Continuing in this vein there is every prospect of genuine sexual liberation — the kind that promotes every level of choice by every individual woman.

Notes

1. Helen Singer Kaplan, *The New Sex Therapy: Active Treatment of Sexual Dysfunctions* (New York: Quadrangle Books 1974).
2. Ibid.
3. Alfred C. Kinsey et al., *Sexual Behavior in the Human Female* (New York: Saunders, 1953).
4. Henry David, *Abortion Research: International Experience* (Lexington, Mass.: Heath, 1974.)
5. Jessie Bernard, *The Future of Motherhood* (New York: Dial, 1977).
6. Ruth Adam, *A Woman's Place: 1910-1975* (New York: Norton, 1975).
7. Don M. Wolfe, *The Image of Man in America* (Dallas: Southern Methodist University Press, 1957); and Susan Brownmiller, *Against Our Will: Men, Women and Rape* (New York: Simon and Schuster, 1975).
8. Michael J. Goldstein and Harold S. Kant with John J. Hartman, *Pornography and Sexual Deviance* (Berkeley: University of California Press, 1973).
9. Una Stannard, *Woman: An Issue,* ed. Lee R. Edwards, Mary Heath, and Lisa Baskin (Boston: Little, Brown, 1972).
10. Karen DeCrow, *Sexist Justice* (New York: Vintage, 1975).

Chapter 6

THE BIOLOGICAL FUTURE

It could well be that the future of humankind is woman. There is a growing body of scientific evidence that not only is the basic human being a female but that human evolution, if not all animal evolution, has proceeded through the adaptive mutations of the human female. In sharp contradiction to Professor Henry Higgins, who asked, "Why can't a woman be more like a man?" evolutionary progress may well be directed toward making a man more like a woman. There is every scientific indication that if men wish to acquire greater longevity, or even make themselves integral to future society, they will become more like women.

While societies have generally discriminated against women, the evolutionary principle has discriminated in their favor. The biological and genetic knowledge now available to us strongly suggests that the basic human being is female. Instead of Eve being fashioned from Adam's rib, Adam is now regarded as the johnny-come-lately in the Garden of Eden.

What kind of evidence are we talking about? In the main, there is more detailed knowledge about the development of the fetus and the contribution made to that development by each parent. Let us start our brief exploration of the evidence by looking at chromosomes, those complex chemical structures at the core of all but a few cells of the body. Between them, the chromosomes contain all the genetic information the body needs for growth, repair, maintenance, and reproduction.

At conception, every one of us is issued twenty-three pairs of chromosomes, one pair from the mother, one pair from the father. Twenty-two of these pairs contain the biological instructions that endow us with physical and possibly psychological attributes. The twenty-third pair, the so-called sex chromosomes, sets us off on a path leading to femaleness or maleness. The chromosomes that code for maleness are called Y chromosomes; the chromosomes that code for femaleness, X chromosomes.

Every cell in our body (except red blood cells) has twenty-three pairs of chromosomes, but our ovaries and testes contain special cells, sex cells, whose function is to separate our chromosome pairs into single sets. When egg and sperm fuse, these sets join up again to give the new individual the requisite twenty-three pairs. The purpose of this apparently pointless taking-apart-and-putting-together process is to create a new being who is different overall from both parents. That is the whole point of sexual reproduction: it gives infinitely greater possibilities for adaptive change, for evolution, than asexual reproduction.

Until fairly recently, basic statements about gender suggested that being female or male was purely a matter of Xs and Ys. But evidence now suggests that there are at least three other times during our existence in the womb when we might become male or female, despite our Xs and Ys. There is actually a four-stage sequence of sex differentiation during which structural and behavioral changes can occur that contradict the genetic sex of the embryo. What these changes amount to is a greater risk to the course of maleness; unless certain changes are initiated at the proper time by the Y chromosome, the embryo and fetus automatically develop as an apparent female. In other words, the basic human being is female. [1]

At this time, our present level of knowledge in biology, specifically in the study of genetics, suggests instead that when we are "speaking chromosomally," female is the expected outcome. The biological procedures for starting life as a male are really extraordinary, even at the stage of a one-month-old fetus. The twenty-third pair of chromosomes contains the genetic material through which gender is determined. These also incorporate sex-linked abnormalities, which result in hereditary disorders such as color blindness, hemophilia, brain hemispheric dominance, and variations that result in Down's syndrome (Mongolism).

The sex chromosomes are aligned differently for men and women. Women have two X chromosomes; men have one X and one Y chromosome. The X chromosome is the seventh largest chromosome, while the Y chromosome is smaller than the smallest autosome (single chromosome). The size difference allows the female, or X, chromosome to carry several genes; the Y chromosome is known to carry only one structural gene. This condition is responsible for making the female parent the transmitter of sex-linked genes, while the paternal parent can transmit only the masculine sex of the offspring and thus not perpetuate on his son his unique chromosomal or genetic abnormalities. He can transmit these through his daughter, however, as characteristics that may then appear in his grandson. There is no chance, therefore, for a genetic male to escape the misfortune of hereditary defects, even though these are recessive traits. [2] There are, it is believed, about seventy sex-linked traits in the human species, and many of these (it is not known how many) are pathological and recessive. There are also sex-influenced characteristics that appear in male offspring, although they are carried by the female and are not directly linked to sex genes.

The X chromosome is also believed to contain about 5 percent of the DNA of the cell nucleus, which means that the growth and activity in development is somewhat accelerated in cells that have a double-X chromosome.[3] This may account for the fact that girl babies mature physically faster than boys, an advantage that includes speedier maturation of the structures necessary for speech and language learning. Girls also get off to a faster start in kinds of learning that lead to earlier readiness for acquiring reading skills. Studies of sex and IQ differences show, however, that boys catch up to girls by age six. Such differences do not always, or even mostly, relate to biological differences, however, because there are differences between the sexes in opportunities for learning and in reaction and reinforcement of performance behaviors.

The second stage of gender development is marked by differentiation of the gonads into testes or ovaries. There is evidence that the tiny Y chromosome organizes sexual differentiation along the lines of different patterns. During the seventh week after conception, the Y chromosome cell division is speeded up, and the inner portion of the beginning gonad differentiates into a testis. If this differentiation fails to occur, then the gonad proceeds to develop as an ovary. The very presence of the Y chromosome is sufficient to initiate and organize this development. In situations where there are many X chromosomes and only one Y chromosome, that small and genetically overwhelmed piece of living material is sufficient to initiate and organize some testicular development.

In a minority of human beginnings, the process of chromosomal division does not result in a pairing of two chromosomes in the twenty-third set but proceeds with additional X or additional Y chromosomes or a single X with an O chromosome. Such conditions result in pathologies like Down's syndrome (Mongolism), Turner's syndrome and Kleinfelder's syndrome. Although each abnormality is genetically different and is identifiable through genetic analysis of cellular material, the production of androgens manufactured by the differentiated testicular gonads performs a masculinizing function on the formation of the genitalia and even on the developing brain. During the third stage of sexual differentiation, after the gonads are formed, the development of external genitalia into either a clitoris and vaginal opening or a penis occurs. The fourth stage, like the earlier stages, can take either a masculine or a feminine path, even in contradiction to the genetic structure of the new human being.

In a series of repetitive processes at each stage of sexual development, a required level of male hormone production and distribution is the basis for continued development as a male. The basic structure of any fetus is female; only through the addition of the Y chromosome and then the male androgen hormones is the primitive duct system that develops into a sexually identified female (the Millerian duct system) repressed and the male (Wolffian) system developed. Even at the fourth stage of development, the hypothalamus, or basic brain development, can be masculinized in a genetically female fetus if somehow the level of androgens is increased.[4]

In contrast to human behavior, lower animals' behavior is largely based on physiological processes. Thus, experiments with rats and monkeys demonstrate that the increased proportion of male hormones in the unborn or even the adult results in increased aggressive behavior by females and decreased availability for conventional patterns of sexual intercourse. Conversely, a male fetus deprived of androgens develops enlarged breasts and a primitive vagina. On the other hand, a total lack of hormones, as happens to the apparently female child with Turner's syndrome (XO paired chromosomes), results in sterility. Such a person can develop into maturity only by being given estrogen, the female sex hormone. It is through studies of the personality and social development of girls with Turner's syndrome that scientists conclude that behavioral development as a female is not particularly related to hormonal production, in sharp contrast with the male and masculine behavior! In other words, in order to "be more like a man," a woman needs to somehow acquire a heavy complement of testosterone either before she is born or at puberty.

The Basic Human Being

This brief review of the biological bases for gender leads us to the conclusion that the basic human being is female and that the term "mankind" is a misnomer. In contradiction to the literature on evolution that describes the female as a peculiar variant of the species, or the "Adam's rib thesis," the fact that embryos are female leads to another consideration of the origin of the species. Serious, thoughtful, and well-documented studies suggest that humankind is descended from aquatic creatures on their maternal side! In some very obvious ways, this appears to follow easily from our new knowledge of human development, and in other ways is directly derived from the biological specialty of evolutionary studies.

Two evolutionary principles would argue that, for the human being, the woman is the direct focus and initiator of the descent of the species. The first principle is that evolutionary change is a function of species survival. Put another way, species change their physical attributes and even their learning capacities and performance in order to continue to survive as species. Thus, the purpose of the adult is to transmit and protect and thus ensure the next generation.

The second principle of evolution to consider is that the roles of male and female in reproduction for all species in which such distinctions exist require that there be more time and involvement by the female in the reproductive process than by the male. Therefore, numerically, fewer males will suffice for the perpetuation of the species.

While our brief summary of prenatal development supports the first principle, we see later in this chapter that, given the greater biological fragility of the male and the more stable and pacific behaviors of the female that are a consequence of her lack of androgens, changes in the female are more likely to be adaptive to evolutionary necessities.

If we consider these premises appropriate explanations of the evolutionary requirements for males and females, then a truly remarkable answer emerges to the question "What makes a woman?" An even more remarkable answer to the problem of understanding the difference between humans and lower species is found in studying the evolution of woman.

Theories that trace the evolution of humans from brachiating (tree swinging) primates — monkeys and such — face some serious problems in trying to account for the differences in physical size, shape, function, and purpose that distinguishes humans from other primates. There is even more difficulty in trying to account for such unique characteristics as the greater dimorphism, or distinct differentiations of body, between male and female humans in contrast with the similar bodies of males and females among other primates.[5]

Mutations (changes in an organism from one generation to another) are adaptive, and distinctions from lower to higher forms symbolize a kind of physical and perhaps even psychological advantage. We have only to compare the differences between male and female humans and apes to realize that the human female is more distinguished from her ape gender peer than is the human male from his. Unlike popular conceptions of women's hair, breasts, and fat layer and distribution as having evolved to afford greater sexual attraction for mate selection, these distinctive body mutations were adaptive for an aquatic creature. Aquatic survival may have been the "missing link" to the puzzling chain of human evolution, as distinguished from the evolution of other anthropoids. If this is the case, then women are the embodiment of the human distinction.

Let us consider the human female breast. There is more to this uniquely human phenomenon than the enrichment of Hugh Hefner and *Playboy* fortunes. The human breast is the instrument for the sustenance of the helpless and hungry infant. The chimpanzee and the gorilla manage the suckling of their young through paired elongated nipples that, except when lactating, appear little different in the male and female. They have a flat pectoral surface, and the young are able, while grasping the mothers' fur, to receive nourishment even while mommy is swinging from tree branch to tree branch. The "naked ape" cannot provide this support for its young. The grasping reflex that is the basis for learning in the developing ape is soon lost in the repertoire of the human infant. (Why the human would have become naked in the first place if the species had remained in the forests and savannahs has not been thoroughly explained and in itself fits better with a theory of aquatic evolution.)

But wait, another species of mammals has breasts — the sirenians. This marine animal group includes the manatee and the dugong. We cannot argue that the manatee is the "missing link," or even our mammalian ancestor(ress). However, mammalian aquatic survival may, at some time, have been predicated on convex pectoral breasts, smooth skin, and a single offspring at a time. Like humans, sirenians have vestigial hair; and humans, like sirenians, sometimes have webbed feet.[6] Considering that evolution from aquatic beings transpired thousands of years ago, it is not really surprising that only a very small percentage of humans have webbed feet. Nor is it surprising that fewer female children have this "vestigial flesh." Women are the initial mutations in the struggle for species survival and are less likely to manifest recessive genetic characteristics.

Arguments for female primacy in the descent of humankind have by no means been resolved. The data presented here are the arguments of a minority of authorities, but they do account for otherwise mysterious and vaguely explicated facts of our lives.

If we want to support this line of reasoning further, and even if we do not wish to support the thesis but to consider the differential facts of life for human males and females, we must examine the males' biological fragility.

The Weaker of the Species

The chances of conceiving a male child are seemingly fewer. Even hormonal survival as a male seems to be in greater jeopardy than survival as a female. Nonetheless, more male babies are conceived, and live male births are slightly ahead of female births, even though as fetuses males are more susceptible to miscarriage and stillbirth. (The current ratio in the United States is 106 males for every 100 females.) It is probably because so many changes are necessary to produce a male from an essentially female body that malformations among males are common. And current studies indicate that boys are born in worse condition if vital signs of both sexes are measured.

This fragility of the male continues throughout life. Perhaps to the person unfamiliar with health statistics, the idea of masculine fragility combined with a mental image of a muscular six-foot-tall humanoid seems laughable. And when reading the statistics that follow, we can moderate their message by recognizing that the male sex role and masculine gender socialization account for some of the higher morbidity and mortality among men. But let us look at some of the facts of male life.

- Boys mature more slowly and are more vulnerable and perishable than females.

- More males die in every year of life than females.

- The male life span is shorter.

- In the first year of life, 27 percent more males than females die.

- More males die in accidents. From birth to four years of age, three boys die accidentally for every two girls; from ages 15-19, the toll rises to four to one.

- Boys are generally clumsier than girls initially and slower to develop control of hand and body muscles.

- Boys are more likely to have speech problems. One study found that 46 percent of boys and only 28 percent of girls in the first three school grades had articulatory problems or speech defects. Boys who stutter outnumber girls almost four to one. Boys also stutter more severely and are less likely to outgrow the condition. The number of boys who stutter increases with age.

- Thus, with respect to vision, hearing, speech, writing, and manual and physical control and dexterity — all the senses and physical capabilities through which people *learn* — boys are disadvantaged.[7]

As if these were not enough problems for the human male, table 1 details the kinds of genetic misfortunes likely to afflict males.

Table 1
Conditions Linked Largely to Sex Genes Found Mostly in Males

Absence of central incisor teeth
Aldrich's syndrome (chronic eczema, mdddle-ear disease, etc.)
Anhidrotic ectodermal dysplasia (maldevelopment of sweat glands)
Cataract
Cerebellar ataxia (loss of muscle coordination)
Color-blindness, red-green type
Day blindness
Defective hair follicles
Double eyelashes
Epidermal cysts
Glaucoma, juvenile type
Hemophilia
Hurler's syndrome (dwarf stature, bone disease)
Icthyosis (scalelike skin)
Mental deficiency of certain types
Mitral stenosis (stricture of bicuspid valve of the heart)
Myopia
Night blindness
Optic atrophy (wasting of the eye)
Parkinsonism
Peoneal atrophy (wasting of muscles of the legs)
Progressive deafness
Retinal detachment
White occipital lock of hair

The idea that women are weaker because they are smaller is one of the major misconceptions of Western society. Women's smaller size in some societies can be contrasted with the similar size and shape of the sexes in other societies. In Burma, for instance, the ideals of beauty are nearly identical for both sexes. Women's smaller size may also be a product of poorer nutrition. Girl babies in some parts of Africa and Asia are still deprived of adequate nutrition when there are food shortages or many children. Female infanticide continues in many societies, and the nutrition of pregnant women is a decisive factor not only in infant health and maternal mortality but also in the morbidity rates of surviving females. In many societies there are direct relationships between class and female mortality/morbidity and sex-size ratios. As we saw in an earlier chapter, there is little relationship between the work role of women and the stereotype about their smaller and weaker condition. In many parts of the world, women continue to do heavy agricultural work.

The Development of Sexuality

There are physiological differences and differing propensities between males and females. And even if we consider the female as the vehicle for mutations and species survival, there are obviously ways in which males develop particular kinds of adaptability and other abilities that serve survival needs.

We return again to the hormones — those fascinating chemical agents that manage to change, stimulate, and terminate cell growth and development. Hormones are formed by the endocrine or ductless glands, which take materials directly from the bloodstream and release hormones directly into the bloodstream after having manufactured them.

The master switching mechanism for hormonal behavior is the hypothalamus in the mid-brain; it functions as a kind of timing device. The hypothalamus very directly interacts with other parts of the brain wherein impulse, action, motivation, and emotion coordinate. The higher the species of animal, the greater is the function of the cortex in mediating behavior and directing it. In this way, humans are far less directed by hormonal activities than are monkeys or canines. Nonetheless, the presence or absence of particular gonadal hormones or their proportions in combination in the system can account for measurable changes in behavior and propensities in perception, emotion, and even motivation.

Hormones influence the developing fetus and the new infant. Their major impact in the life cycle of the sexual system, however, begins with their prominence during puberty. At the start of puberty, pubescence, there is a major growth spurt, and sexual glands mature; the physiological differences between boys and girls become recognizable. There is no "typical" puberty in girls or boys, although girls characteristically commence the process about two years earlier than boys. This earlier start gives them a temporary maturational advantage over boys. For all human beings, puberty is the time of sexual awakening.

There seems to be a more consistent pattern of development for girls than for boys at this time. The female's ovaries begin to secrete estrogen at about age ten, and they grow rapidly after that. From that time until the beginning of menstruation, the girl's development of breast buds, pubic hair, and widened pelvis and hips increasingly mark her a woman-in-process. The age of the onset of menstruation, the monthly cycle of preparation for conception, has been dropping rapidly as societies become more industrialized and better nourished.[8]

The adolescent girl, although awakened sexually, is not as likely as her male counterpart to experience sexuality. Research findings have not clearly established whether this is because of social learning, restrictions, expectations, and role definitions imposed on girls or whether this is a function of the difference in hormonally induced behaviors.[9] The question whether males are sexually aggressive because they are expected to be so or because their productions of testosterone stimulate sexual aggression also has not been answered completely. Data demonstrate that the timing of the maximal levels of testosterone in the bloodstream and sexual drive states are not directly correlated.

There are probably as many confusions and uncertainties about the sexuality of the adolescent girl/woman as there are about ether waves. Survey studies of female sexual behavior such as the early Kinsey report suggest that girls do not generally engage in masturbatory behavior, sexual experimentation, fantasy to orgasm, or mutual sexual stimulation activities in the way their male age mates are reported to do. If one is to believe the reports, then the path to adult female sexuality is considerably different from that of males and is more likely to be the consequence of learning than of instinctive behaviors. Of course, it may also be a consequence of the difference in the relationship of the mid-brain to the cortex, which is still another distinction between the sexes that exists before birth or shortly afterward. Certainly, considerable data demonstrate differences by sex in perceptual processes and possibly even in the experience of various sensations. Whatever the ultimate answer to the biological mysteries of female development into sexuality, by the time of adolescence an enormous weight of social and psychological factors is at work, especially in the sex-role impositions.

Will Men Be More Like Women?

In Bali, the concept of human beauty idealizes the same body proportions for men and women, and there is a striking similarity of appearance between the sexes. There are no genuine historic data on how many generations of Balinese have persisted in this aesthetic, but the fact suggests an evolutionary change process based on selection that has greatly modified the relative distributions of muscle and body fat and even suggests hormonal modifications in conjunction with behavioral changes.

As mate selection may well proceed in accordance with species survival, the outcome of values both economic and aesthetic depends on increasing fine motor coordination, intellectual flexibility, language facility, and cooperation. There is thus every reason to believe that there will be less aesthetic value associated with the physical differences between men and women.

There are alternatives to this prognosis. If male humans prove unadaptable for maximizing species survival and if they persist in valuing aggression and conventional macho wisdom, there may be no human race at all.

Notes

1. John Money and Anke Ehrhardt, *Man and Woman/Boy and Girl* (New York: Signet, 1974).
2. Ibid.
3. Clarice Stasz Stoll, *Female and Male: Socialization, Social Roles and Social Structure* (Dubuque, Iowa: William C. Brown, 1978).
4. Ibid.
5. Elaine Morgan, *The Descent of Woman* (New York: Stein and Day, 1972).
6. Patricia Cayo Sexton *The Feminized Male* (New York: Random House, 1969).
7. Ibid., 197.
8. Dirk L. Schaeffer, ed., *Sex Differences in Personality: Readings* (Belmont, Calif.: Brooks/Cole, 1971).
9. Ibid.

Chapter **7**   WHAT DO WOMEN WANT?

Several years ago, behavioral psychologists experimenting with chimpanzees provided token rewards for those who learned to push certain levers. In exchange for the tokens, the anthropoids were able to obtain grapes and other favorite fruits. First one female and then the others discovered that they could obtain the tokens earned by their male companions through providing sexual gratification. Soon the male chimps were working very hard to obtain more and more tokens, and the experimenters realized that the female chimpanzees were getting all the fruit!

The economics of prostitution are often used to illustrate the degradation of women in societies that limit their access to equality. But the marketplace economics of sexuality reflect instead another dimension of the sex-role relationships of the rest of that society. If women are slaves on the basis of sex or race or conquest, their place in the market is determined by their attributes for that marketplace. If sexuality is a commodity, then women (and, in some instances, men) become sexual objects and tokens for exchange.

Solon, who with his legal system disfranchised Athenian women, also established the first house of prostitution that came under official government protection.

Socialists have pointed out the relationship between economic dependence and oppression. Apart from the rhetorical value of such arguments and the obvious ideological rationalization they provide, there is considerable anthropological, archaeological, and historical evidence that placing women in a condition of dependence by limiting their economic opportunities and responsibilities is a corollary of oppression, but there may be some question as to which sex is thereby the most oppressed. Perhaps one of the earliest and most poignant feminist protests was uttered by Medea:

> Ay, of all living and of all reasoning things
> Are women the most miserable race:
> Who first needs buy a husband at great price
> To take them for owner of our lives:
> For this ill is more keen than common ills. . . .

For evil-famed to women is divorce,
Nor can one spurn a husband. She so brought
Beneath new rule went . . . had surely need
To be a prophetess, useless at home
She learned the likeliest prospect with her spouse. . . .

But, say they, we, while they fight with a spear,
Lead in our homes a life undangerous:
Judging amiss; for I would liefer thrice
Bear brunt of arms than once bring forth a child.[1]

At its most basic level, feminism insists that women's economic, political, and social lives be determined by attributes other than their procreative functions. It is obvious that such consideration has been limited in many spheres, but nowhere can this be more damaging to the objective of equality than in the economic system.

Insofar as the political system determines property rights, it predicates the relative status of the sexes. For this reason, women directed their efforts to obtaining the vote in Western societies. Socialist ideologies promised equality. In most instances they fulfilled this promise during their revolutionary period by a heavy representation of women on governing committees and decision-making bodies to assure their equipotentiality in the system. The early impetus was not continued, however.

In Sri Lanka, and in some groups in Southeast Asia and Africa (e.g., Sierra Leone and Ghana), women have traditionally monopolized commerce and thus controlled the monetary exchange and fiscal practices of their societies. Such advantagement has not necessarily carried with it political and economic equality. In rural societies women have had, and continue to have, responsibility within the home and in production. While they may be able to squirrel away the "egg money" and thus maintain some discretionary funds, more often their venue of discretion has demanded the ultimate measure of effort from their already worn bodies and exhausted spirits. The toll on rural women is reflected in health statistics on the least industrialized countries and parts of nations. These show that, on average, such women live no longer than men in their society and sometimes not as long. This is remarkable in view of the natural physiological advantage women have for longevity. Women residing in cities tend to have a slightly better life expectancy. This, in itself, is one of the most convincing proofs of vital distinctions between economic sciences in relation to women. Other official data are even more dramatic evidence of the hazards to women's physical well-being and even survival resulting from women's inequality.[2]

Women constitute half of the world's population and a third of its workforce. They perform two-thirds of the total work hours but receive only one-tenth of the world's income. They probably possess less than one-hundredth of world assets. Throughout the world, woman-headed households constitute the majority of the poverty population.[3] As the world moves into a time of slower economic growth and higher technology the market for the labor-intensive productions of the less developed labor force declines. Women, who are the majority of participants in these industries, have little to look forward to.

Women in more industrialized societies are "protected" by legislation passed at an earlier time to assure their health and safety. At present they are victimized through these prohibitions in employment by being unable to enter some better-paying occupations.

The International Labour Organization and other functioning bodies of the UN are attempting to present recommendations to the member states to influence the provision of equal opportunities for women in the workplace, in part through focusing on such topics as "Workers with Family Responsibilities." The deputy director general of the ILO points out the paradox that "women are not permanently in the *official* work force and yet they are working *permanently.*" Women's participation in remunerated employment has been on the increase. Also increasingly, governments are placing equality of opportunity, training, and salary on their statute books.[4]

It is not surprising under the conditions of women's labor in rural societies that throughout Europe and North America, at least, and possibly in the rest of the world as well, women, more than men, migrate to urban centers. In some countries where rural life is particularly hard on women and where emigration visas are readily obtained, more women emigrate than men. This has been the case for Irish women for the past two hundred years.

There are many ways to study the impact and interaction of women with economic systems and circumstances. Having briefly reviewed the international perspective, we now consider some of the specifics at various points of this interface.

Socialization and the Economic System

Without entering the battle between ideologies on economic determinism, it is obvious that the economic system surrounds and overlays the socialization process. Consider the model in figure 1 as a two-dimensional portrayal of the process and dynamics operating to shape young members of the

Figure 1

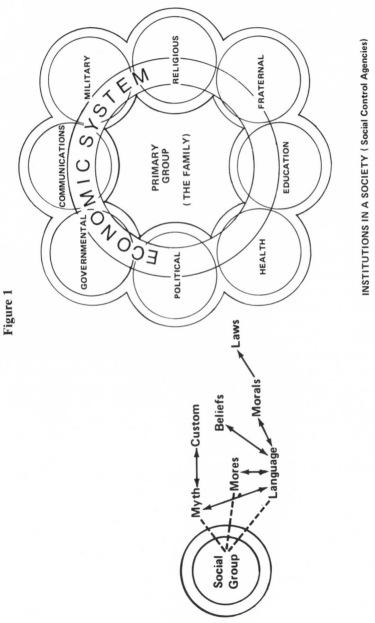

INSTITUTIONS IN A SOCIETY (Social Control Agencies)

Social Control Agencies

informal ----------

direct ⟶

group and segregate those members who do not fit into the social system. All the institutions of society — education, health, fraternal, religious, and so forth — serve in this program as agents of the legal system operating through the economic system.

In most societies today (and for generations past) girl babies are treated differentially by every institution with which they have contact from birth through adulthood. The customs, mores, and belief systems — even the languages of these societies — incorporate the idea of biological determinism into their fabric and through that ideology restrict female children to a limited repertoire of role behaviors, aspirations, and acceptable models and responses. Children who do not conform are either cast out of the institutions or put into an intensive retraining program.

Socialization happens within the family unit as well as through the institutions. The child, as part of a family that is either conventional or alien to the society, evolves his or her identity from that relationship too. Still other socializing experiences derive from the climate within the family constellation. Running like a constant through all these dynamic interactions is the economic identity of the growing individual and the family. Sometimes this is reflected through social class, which in many societies indexes family wealth, access to political power, and behavioral standards for the children as youngsters and their probable place as adults. This is dramatically presented in the ornamentation of daughters in many societies. Some African groups place metal rings around the necks of their daughters in numbers proportionate with the family's economic status; other groups do tattoos relative to the same criteria. Asian and European societies have long regarded the clothing and jewelry of wives and daughters as symbols of the father's or husband's economic niche.

Where dowries or bride-prices are the norm, females from their earliest awareness must recognize their predicament as commodities — perhaps highly valued or perhaps valued only so long as their virginity is intact.

Some may argue that the bride-price provides assurance that the girl will be valued and cared for. True, in groups that consider the female human being an object or lacking the immortal soul vouchsafed to males, the man who has had to work very hard for several years to "pay" for his wife may treat her with greater care than that bestowed on the household cat.

Americans and Western Europeans may feel far removed from such pecuniary practices. Nevertheless, the conventional wedding in Western society is replete with the symbolism of bride-price, dowry, and marriage by capture. Little girls, raised to dream of themselves as traditional brides, fantasize the diamond engagement ring their suitor will present. Isn't this a bride-price? They imagine the glorious wedding, the splendid gown, their attendants, and the trousseau provided, of course, by the bride's family. Is this not a dowry of sorts? Then the capture scene. The bride is brought to the ritual by her family, from whom the groom takes her off on a "honeymoon," usually leaving the festivities surreptitiously or with shouts and showers of fertility symbols. With all these exchanges of symbolized wealth, the husband has taken ownership of the bride from her father, who "gave her away" at the altar.

The Value of a Woman

The last verses in the book of Proverbs catalog the "qualities of a good wife" — but these verses describe a woman "of valor" who engages in commerce, industry, agriculture, and charity and deals wisely and justly with her family and community. We are told:

> . . . her price is far above rubies. . . .

> Strength and dignity are her clothing;
> And she laugheth at the time to come. . . .

> Grace is deceitful, and beauty is vain; . . .

> And let her works praise her in the gates.[5]

But, in fact, almost universally in today's world, women's work is little valued and is certainly not compensated "above rubies." Housework is not compensated at all, and invariably when the issue is raised, there are giggles and laughter. On an urgent note, the value of a woman's work is not recognized in the survivor benefits provided her widower and children if she dies. Social welfare systems do not incorporate women who have performed "women's work" into their retirement benefits. Women who spend their years as houseworkers to their husbands and children are not necessarily eligible for half the property if the couple divorce. Ironically, it has been in the few cases of compensation for "palimony," or sharing a household outside of marriage, that a woman has been compensated for the sacrifice of her own career in order to meet the requirements of her "pal's" career. There is no such provision for wives.

Before we examine the hard, cold statistics of women's participation in the workforce and the barriers to her achievement of economic equity in the workplace, perhaps the most illustrative statement about "women's work" was quoted by Jan Myrdal in *Report from a Chinese Village*. Li Yin-hua, secretary of the Liu Ling People's Commune in Shensi, China, said:

> Thirty years ago, the emancipation of women was one of the main points in our programme. We sang songs about it. I can still remember them. We had a slogan: "Free their feet!" Now their feet are free and women can work in the fields, so now both men and women share in cultivating the land. Thirty years ago we were saying "Let both men and women take part in our revolution," and now that has come about. . . . Marriage is free now, too. . . . Women are hard workers. Do you see those women down there have baskets beside them as they weed, but the men don't? That's because the women aren't only weeding, they are also collecting grass for the family's pigs.[6]

While values, ideologies, and cultures change, women's work is universally recognized as necessary to the operation of the society — but it is not recognized for compensation. As George Bernard Shaw said, the only way for a woman to provide for herself is to be good to some man who can be good to her. His remark complemented George Eliot's observation: "We don't ask what a woman does, we ask whom she belongs to."

In the Workforce

Women work in their homes unpaid and outside their homes on a wage basis in increasing numbers and for more years of their lives. There are a few women in the upper executive echelons and some women in the better-paid, higher-status professions like law and medicine. But the largest concentrations of women are in the lower service occupations, such as nursing and household work; or they are factory operatives, waitresses, and beauticians; or in the lower-paid professions, such as teaching in elementary and secondary schools, librarians; or in salesclerking and office work. The more significantly female the labor force in an occupation, the more likely that the entire occupation is lower paid than another group that has predominantly male workers with the same educational and training requirements.

As candidates for jobs, women have been unlikely to be considered on their professional merits. Realization of these facts has led to equal opportunities legislation and monitoring systems, advocacy, and inservice training programs. Such programs are in place in most countries now, with a wide range of results. In developing countries, the increased participation by women in the technologically developing workforce has often meant less support and protection for the health of women and their children rather than advantagement in living standards.

Most of the women in the labor force are married, and many of them are mothers. In fact, according to a 1978 survey of workers in Great Britain, there were as many married women as married men in the labor force. As for work preparation, an even higher number of girls passed their "A" levels than did boys, and at the "O" levels, there were equal numbers of boys and girls who passed. Differences in career preparations really turn up in the postsecondary phase when twenty times more females than males opt for secretarial courses and 52 percent more males than females opt for degree courses. As we see in chapter 9, that is a clear consequence of sex-role socialization differences supported and perhaps initiated in educational institutions.

Studies of gross earnings by sex show that in the United States, the United Kingdom, and the EEC countries women as a group earn about 74 percent of the amount earned by men. This is a striking gain by women and was accomplished during the 1970s. At the start of that decade, women commonly grossed about 50 percent of men's earnings. As a corollary, however, none of these countries has enrolled as high as 50 percent of the women in institutions of higher education. This points to a grim prospect for evening out men's and women's places on the scale of gross earnings.

There was a time in Western societies when the socioeconomic status and income of a family was inversely proportional to employed wives. Now the relationship is the opposite. At the bottom of the income ladder, of course, we find employed wives and mothers or single women heads of households, but from the next income level up through the top, there is a steady incremental *increase* in the proportion of working wives. Another interesting sidelight on these households is that they tend to have fewer children as well as higher incomes. Birthrates bear no direct relationship to the total proportion of women in the labor force, paid or unpaid, but they do bear an inverse relationship to the level of income and status of job.

Efforts, public and private, to establish day-care programs and child-care systems have been made only sporadically. Various model programs and initiatives evolve from time to time in prominent workplaces or under the direction of child specialists at various institutions for higher education or research, but thus far, child-care arrangements in the Western world are made by individuals and with individuals. One study in the United States indicated that the majority of children cared for outside their homes were cared for by unlicensed, untrained individuals. Other studies have shown that licensed, trained child-care workers in established day-care facilities might not be providing sufficient stimulation or positive reinforcements for the children under their care.[7] Still other surveys find that children in day-care facilities are in serious danger of contracting hepatitis, ear infections, and other contagions. In kibbutzim in Israel, where workers are highly trained and supervised, consultant services are provided and facilities are well planned and thought out. Nonetheless, parents are beginning to assert demands for increasing the proportion of the day when they will take personal responsibility for their children.

Although every EEC country, the United States, and Canada have reported increases in the number of mothers of infants to three-year-old children in the workforce, few have provided appropriate numbers of places in child-care facilities for that increase. Many governments, such as the Republic of Ireland, provide child care for that age group only if there is serious family disturbance and only for the most extreme cases.

There seems to be a tacit assumption in many societies (and even a formal arrangement in the People's Republic of China) that women's participation in the labor force is complemented and extended by the work of the grandmother in providing child care for the mother. Moreover, considerable effort is made to remind women that they should be the primary caretakers of their infants and very young children. Nevertheless, only three Western European governments have incorporated into their affirmative action programs provisions for paid maternity leaves and nursing breaks that would facilitate the mother's remaining the primary caretaker while in the workforce. On a more subtle level, it is apparent that creches are provided for women to attend religious services and for women employees in many status occupations in the United States and Western Europe. The U.S. Department of Labor Women's Bureau has provided, in its headquarters building, a facility for the children of their employees; the U.S. Senate and House of Representatives also have provided a day-care center for some of the children of their staff. But it is highly unlikely that a department store or automobile factory would house children of their employees during the parents' workday.

There is continuous evidence of discrimination in training, salaries, promotions, hiring, and conditions of employment, as well as continuing evidences of violations of legal codes supposed to provide, monitor, and enforce equal opportunities. If there is a loophole of any sort in any part of the machinery, it is certain that it is utilized maximally. Every suspected weakness in the fabric of the affirmative action program is tried and tested. But there have been some recognizable improvements. Kate Millett's cataloging of the failures of the U.S. 1964 Civil Rights Act in providing genuine equal opportunities for American women has only to be compared with the reports on the UN Decade for Women Programme of Action presented at the 1980 conference in Copenhagen for indications of change.[8]

Women's achievement in the economic sphere, however, directly confronts the political question of feminism as a revolution or the women's movement as evolution. If the feminist revolution is to prevail, then its first target for change is the extant economic system, through which all other institutions may be changed. If the objective of the women's movement is the prevailing current of the future, then the objective for change is the inclusion of women in every echelon of the economic system and in every role capacity. That would transform the economic system from its service in the continued oppression of women to the service of people regardless of gender.

Women United — A Brief History

The current of the women's movement catalyzed in the 1960s when, in America and Europe, several other movements dealing with economic equity and identity gained momentum. The student protests of the period, as well as ethnic and peace movements, included women at every level except leadership for most of the time and in most places. Earlier attempts by women to unite in a women's movement showed mixed results.

Eighteenth-century republicanism, which reached a kind of fruition in the formation of the United States of America, the French Revolution, and the failed Irish rebellion, brought into communication feminist thinkers on both sides of the Atlantic. But that was not enough to spark a women's movement. Abigail Adams, Mary Wollstonecraft, Catherine Macauley, Mme. Roland, and Judith Sargent Murray are today recognized as feminists because, as writers, they left a record of their thoughts and because in their lifetimes they drew serious critical reaction to the ideas they communicated. They were intellectual children of the republican thesis — the Rights of Man — as articulated by Thomas Paine, or the anarchist philosophy of William Godwin and the humanism of Mill and Locke. These forces also gave rise to a convergent force vaguely audible in the Ireland and England of the late eighteenth century — the labor movement.

The guild system of the Middle Ages not only included women but often had women in positions of leadership and authority. By the eighteenth century and the industrial revolution, this had changed considerably. Although women continued in the industrial labor force they, along with journeymen and apprentices, were no longer in the guilds at all. Guild masters established wages and conditions of employment that deliberately excluded anyone who participated in trade union organization. At the turn of the century in Britain, the Wilberforce bill, which became the Combination Act, made unions and unionizing a crime with punishments that were severely enforced. The law in Ireland was twice as severe in its punitive prescriptions. The act was repealed in 1824. By that time, the cause of labor unionization had become entwined in Ireland with the cause of Irish freedom.

It was Irish immigrant labor in the factories of Manchester and Lancashire that caught the attention of Frederick Engels, communist ideologist and textile manufacturer. He drew from this acquaintance no doubt when he wrote his profeminist treatise *The Family, Private Property and the State.*[9] This work apparently brought together for the first time the connections between women's status, the economic system, the plight of labor, and the philosophy of communism, although, by the time of its publication, other activists and intellectuals in Britain and America were working in the nexus of these movements.

The earlier women's movement in America was closely intertwined with the movement to abolish slavery. Unlike the women's suffrage movement in twentieth-century Ireland, whose adherents also espoused Irish nationalism, republicanism, and trade unionism, and sometimes socialism as well, their sisters in America only intermittently incorporated the cause of labor or socialism into the mainstream of their movement. And American women who were staunch abolitionists also were likely to employ immigrant girls (often Irish) as menials at very low wages and very great condescension.

An international tone in the campaign for women's equality was established for European and American women through contacts made at the World Anti-Slavery Convention in 1840, the International Socialist and Labour Congress that took place in the second half of the nineteenth century, and the international activities of family planning organizations. These causes were intertwined, and leadership was often interchangeable.

The Seneca Falls convention of 1848, with its Declaration of Sentiments, marked the end of the first phase in the women's movement to equality. During the convention, American women and their European counterparts attempted to raise the consciousness of other women through identifying with them and arguing against the artificial limits on women's activities.

Different issues became the catalysts that brought women to a consciousness of their disadvantagement. During much of the eighteenth and nineteenth centuries, individuals became militant out of their personal frustration in one or another dimension of their lives. Most of the conflict experienced by upper- and middle-class women derived from their lack of property rights. This affected them in two especially odious ways. First, unlike men of their class, upper-class women who were property owners lacked representation; second, married women lost all recourse to legal redress or adult treatment. Married women had no right to the property they owned prior to marriage and no control over their own earnings during marriage. It was apparent that the key to their predicament was obtaining the vote.

The Manchester Women's Suffrage Committee was founded in 1867 by Lydia Becker. Within a year, more than 5000 women had become members of the association, and in 1869 unmarried women householders in the United Kingdom were given the right to vote in local elections. As middle-class women moved into the workforce as nurses, teachers, and office workers, they exerted more pressure for suffrage.

Meanwhile, lower-class British women became more directly involved in the struggle for workers' rights. But the Women's Trade Union League (which became the National Federation of Women Workers) did not really get off the ground until the turn of the century, under the leadership of Mary MacArthur.

The rapid industrialization that changed the nature of the family in England also changed the social organization and political structure of other Western European countries during the second half of the nineteenth century. Sweden, for instance, experienced severe population displacements with many more women than men moving into the major city, Stockholm, while large numbers of farm families emigrated to America. Young women came to the city because their families could no longer support them, and at the same time they were legally barred from paid employment. The early Swedish women's rights organizations fought for women's paid employment while their colleagues in England and America were fighting for the vote. Fredrika Brenner and Ellen Key came into confrontation with the Lutheran church, to which 90 percent of the Scandinavian population belonged, which was rigidly opposed to sexual freedom and the equality of the sexes in marriage. Key's advocacy of free motherhood was consistent with the traditional rural practices of "trial marraiges" wherein the formal religious commitment was taken only after evidence of pregnancy. In 1915, feminist legislation and a welfare system emerged together within five years. The changes were made in the definition of the family, divorce, and marriage laws, and the access of women to education and employment. In the years since, education has proceeded on an androgynous sex-role basis, and sexuality is accepted as an individual matter.[10]

It is of interest to note that while in Europe and America the nineteenth century marked a new era of struggle toward women's economic and political equality, the same century witnessed the demise in Africa of women's access to political power. In precolonial tribal societies there had been many traditions of female innovation, leadership, and authority. Some groups continue to mark their descent through their maternal families even to this day. For the most part, however, the occupation and colonization of Africa by European powers destroyed many of the social forms as well as ethnic units, and the resulting perversion of African society has never been disentangled.

The women's movement in America proceeded along a different path and with many regional variations. The newer western states of the United States granted women voting rights immediately. The industrial North and Northeast were socially and politically closer to conditions in England. The largely rural, slaveholding South was more resistant, yet many leaders of the women's movement were born and raised in the South, including the former slave, Sojourner Truth, whose "Ain't I a Women?" reminded middle-class white feminists that black women in America suffered from a double oppression.

Many leaders of the American women's suffrage movement came out of Protestant evangelism, which called for reform in the religious sphere as well as for a moral crusade against slavery, intemperance, and the degradation of the industrial working class. Some of the later leaders of the women's movement were closely related by blood or marriage. Although many of their husbands shared the women's commitment to the ideals of equality, most of the women found it impossible to sustain their struggle for freedom in conjunction with a traditional or conventional family. The Blackwell sisters, whose brothers were married to prominent suffragists, never married. Instead, they informally adopted children, sometimes immigrant children, whom they raised as domestics. Elizabeth Blackwell was the first American women physician and a campaigner for women's access into the medical profession and higher education.

The split between the mainstream of the women's suffrage movement in America and women labor unionizers in the end defused women's efforts and delayed the granting of women's suffrage until the Nineteenth Amendment was passed in 1920. In the last quarter of the nineteenth century the suffrage leaders were middle class, respectable, and had friends in high places. The working women, on the other hand, were associated with the turmoil and violence of the labor movement, and although the number of women workers increased by the turn of the century, the focus of the women's suffrage movement was oriented toward education and property rights. They devoted their efforts (successfully) to securing voting rights in the newer states and achieved their goal of admitting women into institutions of higher education, sometimes course by course.

Carrie Chapman Catt took over the leadership of the National American Women Suffrage Association from an exhausted Susan B. Anthony in 1900. By that time, Anthony and Elizabeth Stanton had visited Britain and begun the international women's suffrage movement as the International Council of Women, which held congresses in 1888, 1893, and 1903. In 1904, in Berlin, the International Women Suffrage Alliance was launched with eight affiliates in Australia, Denmark, Germany, Great Britain, Netherlands, Norway, Sweden, and the United States. Carrie Chapman Catt remained the leader of the alliance until 1923.

Women in the United Kingdom were not granted equal franchisement until the Equal Franchise Act of 1928 — eight years after their American sisters and ten years after the vote had been granted to U.K. women over age thirty. The women's suffrage movement in England had been more concentrated and intensive over a shorter period of time but with a more unified constituency that incorporated issues across class lines by the time of the First World War.

Mary Wollstonecraft's early efforts notwithstanding, it was 1869 before a document on women's equality caught the attention and commitment of men and women who would organize around it. That text was John Stuart Mill's *The Subjection of Women*. The spark for the movement can be traced to many factors in the rapidly industrializing England of the late nineteenth century, but there were also individuals whose efforts and innovative imaginations raised women's consciousness. Emmaline Pankhurst was one of these leaders. She married into a family with a strong history of radical and women's suffrage activists. She and her husband were socialists who joined the Independent Labor party in 1894, and she worked on the School Board and the Board of Guardians by serving on the Education Committee, since she could not be elected to the board itself. With Ann Kenney, Pankhurst and her daughters, Sylvia and Christabel, formed the militant Women's Social and Political Union in 1903. Two years later, Christabel and Ann Kenney were arrested for causing a disturbance at a political meeting. This seemed to set the tone for activists for the next decade. During this period, the police brutally clubbed women demonstrating for their rights and imprisoned many of them under such terrible conditions that in 1909 imprisoned suffragists went on a hunger strike. At first, women were released when they became weakened by hunger, but as the government's position hardened against the demonstrators, they started force feeding the women, which aroused public sympathies in behalf of the suffragists.

The women's movement in Britain and America did not go underground after women were granted voting rights, but large-scale support for equal access to economic equity seemed to subside. The convergence of social and political liberation struggles internationally during the 1960s once again provided a climate conducive to an assessment of women's status. As we see in the next chapter, the current focus, thrust, and direction of the women's movement has capitalized on political gains made by the earlier movement for women's enfranchisement in seeking the fulfillment of the original objective — economic equity.

Notes

1. Euripedes, *Medea.*
2. International Labor Organization, *Report to the United Nations Mid-Decade Conference on the Status of Women* (Copenhagen, 1980)
3. Jessie Bernard, *The Female World* (New York: Macmillan, 1981).
4. ILO report.
5. Proverbs, "The Value of a Woman."
6. Jan Myrdal, *Report from a Chinese Village* (Pittsburgh: KNOW, monograph, 1970).
7. "Who Shall Care for Our Children? The History and Development of Day Care in the United States," in *Women, a Feminist Perspective,* ed. J. Freeman (Palo Alto, Calif.: Mayfield, 1975).
8. United Nations Mid-Decade Program of Action, August 1980.
9. Frederich Engels, *The Origin of the Family, Private Property, and the State* (New York: International Publishers, 1972).
10. Elina Avio-Mamila, "Sex Role Attitudes in Finland, 1966-1970," *Journal of Social Issues* 28 (1972): 93-110.

Chapter **8**   THE NEW FEMINISTS

The women's movement of the late twentieth century and the reactivation of feminism did not erupt by spontaneous combustion, nor were they consequences (as one revisionist history suggests) of the suburban housewife malaise articulated by Betty Friedan in *The Feminine Mystique*.[1]

The barricades that remained in place against women's equality became more starkly dramatic in a landscape that gradually was bereft of barricades. Simone de Beauvoir[2] called attention to the unfinished revolution that had been distracted into the Anglo-American middle-class suffrage movement and then muted into oblivion when this fraction of the world's population of women achieved the right to vote. The groundswell of the campaign for women's rights seemed to have been siphoned off into several directions and then to have trickled underground.

The women's movement of the late nineteenth and early twentieth centuries was characterized by divisions emanating from geographic, economic, and class priorities and distinctions. When women failed to become more conscious of their commonalities, working-class women focused their energies on improving the lot of the worker through labor organizations, middle-class women believed that political power inhered in obtaining voting rights, and women in socialist countries oriented themselves to the revolutionary class struggle in the assumption that improvements in women's lot would follow from it.

The phenomenal bonding of women again in the 1960s was, in Western countries, a consequence of their coming together in the new suburbia and within the pressure cooker of the ethos of "family togetherness." For rural women in underdeveloped countries, the mid-twentieth century marked the migration of their menfolk to new cities or as guest workers to foreign countries. The distance between the haves and have-nots among nations was overshadowed by a new segregation of the sexes: men struggled on competitive economic scenes, and women were left alone to contend with childbearing and child rearing and years of frustrated talents and misspent energies.

Having sounded the early warning system about women's malaise, Friedan raised the same shibboleths for its solution as had been attempted with

104

limited success by the earlier women's suffrage movement. Women should work together with men as partners to achieve the goals of women's equality. Friedan said that in 1973 in an opening speech to the international audience at the first feminist planning conference, and she said it again eight years later in her book *The Second Stage.*[3]

There is little doubt that Friedan has articulated the most controversial issues associated with the women's movement of the last century or the present one. These issues, put most directly, are, first, the nature of the women's struggle — is it revolutionary or evolutionary? Is it intended to put women alongside men, as a kind of change of faces in the same system, or is it intended to change the system? Second, can women change their status without recognizing their common class character?

The modern women's movement marks the reemergence, not the invention, of feminism. Nineteenth-century women rebelled against the social and political oppression they found directed at women; they also formed efficient and powerful organizations in order to gain some degree of equality for females. And of course, in even earlier centuries, lone voices from different cultures protested against the lowly and restricting status accorded to women.

Nevertheless, it was during the nineteenth century that feminist thoughts first lit the bonfire of a popular movement. How does the memory of that upsurge of feminism affect today's women's movement?

First, both movements marked a change in women's consciousness. There was a realization that women, individually and collectively, *could* make an impact on the social and political system. The plain fact is that full humanity — the realization of the human potential — calls for the right and the capacity to make choices. The right of choice is, universally, the philosophical, political, and theological basis for suffrage, citizenship, and service. Almost universally, however, women were denied this basic right — they had no vote and no political or economic power. They lived restricted lives, the conditions of which were beyond their control. The development of feminist movements, therefore, marked not only women's desire to improve the quality of their lives but, just as important, their eagerness to assume social and political responsibilities, to become involved in the almost exclusively male "public" world. Largely through feminist movements, women came to think of themselves as people with power and as citizens in the fullest sense of the word.

To illustrate this point, let us look at two groups of contemporary women whose involvement in feminist activity and social action has never attracted · sensational journalism but nevertheless has marked a huge change in women's attitudes and behavior. The first group consists of women who thought of themselves primarily as housewives and who accepted the sex-role socialization norms handed on to them. They were slow to identify with the women's movement. This fact can be attributed as much to their alienation from political participation — their assumption that they were people who reacted rather than acted — as to their distrust of change. The second groups consists of women in low-paid "women's jobs." Before legislation forced employers to go part of the way toward elimination of sex discrimination in wages and opportunities, these women saw no chance of improving their lot.

Neither group identified with militant spokeswomen of the women's movement. But as feminist ideas filtered through the culture, members of both groups began to examine their discontents. When office workers joined the women's movement and factory workers through their unions demanded the same pay and pension benefits as their male colleagues enjoyed, it indicated not only an identification with the struggle for equality but also a signal that they had begun to realize their political efficacy. The same process can be observed when "token" women executives and professionals formed peer groups that cut across job status and encompassed other women employees. Out in the suburbs, housewives came together to share their discontents; and parent-teacher associations and women's organizations took concerted action on issues affecting their neighborhoods.

As all such activities attest, women have come to recognize their common situation and to affirm their strength. By cooperating with one another, women have broken many of the barriers that patriarchal tradition erected between them for purposes of manipulation and isolation.

In both the earlier and contemporary women's movements, then, bonding and cooperation between women has been an essential driving force. There are some striking differences, however, in the goals and strategies employed by the two movements. Most important, perhaps, is the fact that the current women's movement is multifaceted, multifocused, and multi-purpose. In contrast, the earlier movement focused on the vote as the issue of central importance to women. There were many dissenting voices to that policy, but they tended not to be heard.

Another area of difference between the two movements concerns women's sexuality. Where the earlier movement had viewed sexuality as a male force, dangerous and destructive to women, today's feminists are much more interested in exploring the nature and potential of female sexuality. Contemporary demands for female sexual autonomy and for a woman's right to have full control over her reproductive function would have shocked many of the earlier feminists; indeed, their view might well have been that such demands were a betrayal of women's "natural purity."

Other major differences can be found in styles of organization and methods of communication and protest. Some suffragists resorted to illegal and "antisocial" actions in pursuing the suffrage campaign; they burned letters in mailboxes, ripped Old Masters in art galleries; and chained themselves to railings. But most feminists of the time expressed their views conventionally in writing and in lectures — in the same manner, in fact, as men were accustomed to agitate for social and political reform. A small number of organizer feminists used personal discussion as a means of raising political consciousness. For example, Mother Jones (May Harris) and Elizabeth Gurley Flynn gained the support of women workers and the wives of miners, laborers, and the unemployed by discussing their common suffering and experience with them.

At the beginning of the current movement for women's equality, however, strategies and tactics deliberately ran counter to man-made expectations of political protest. Such tactics often resulted in utterly confounding the establishment and winning considerable victories. In the spring of 1971, for example, the Harvard University Women's Collective took over a university-owned building. The building had been given to them for use as a women's center, but within a short time the university decided to sell it instead. A large number of women occupied the building and stayed there for a week. They neither elected leaders nor appointed "official" spokeswomen — a fact that puzzled and enraged university authorities. No one knew how many women were in the collective at any one time. No one involved in the occupation of the building knew the surnames of the others unless they were previously acquainted. Women came and went; the building was never empty. Inside were women and children, posters and photographs, and much excited talk. Animated discussion and optimistic speculation were punctuated by laughter. When the courts ordered the women out, they refused to obey.

The sheriff's forces arrived, surrounded the building, and using bullhorns, demanded that the women leave. After a week, the women collectively decided that they would evacuate the building, but they dictated the terms of their compliance. They had tasted the power of self-determination and were in no mood for surrender.

Many other radical movements of the 1960s began as unstructured groups but fairly early on lapsed into the old leadership-followers pattern. The establishment of hierarchies and procedures resulted in the formation of elite groups within these movements — elites that then easily became targets for cooption by the institutions against which they had arrayed themselves. Leaders lost credibility with their constituents, and the latter, often frustrated and alienated, lost their cohesion and their potential for political strength.

Differently again from their predecessors in the earlier women's movement, contemporary feminists have consistently stressed the importance of organizing themselves separately from men. For example, NOW started out as the National Organization *of* Women, and some felt that its feminist identity was undermined when it became the National Organization *for* Women. Many of the women who formed the nucleus of the new women's movement in America had been through the radical and civil rights struggle of the early 1960s in tandem with male colleagues. Their feminist consciousness was raised during that period largely because the men with whom they worked consigned them to "women's work" and excluded them from decision-making positions — in much the same way that their more conservative sisters were excluded from the boardrooms of ITT and IBM. When an internationally recognized black civil rights leader said that "the place for women is prone," and when others expressed it only slightly differently as "women's place is under men," women began to organize for themselves.

The principal organizing vehicle of the 1960s and 1970s was the "consciousness-raising session." Other 1960s radicals had taken their signal from the sociologist C. Wright Mills[4] and had developed political insights from personal experience. Radical women who were turning to feminism formed women-only consciousness-raising groups as a necessary first step to freeing themselves from sexist pressures, values, and assumptions. Because sexism, like racism, is the taken for granted, unexamined standard of all individuals socialized into most societies, women had to become intensely sensitized to their condition in order to see clearly what had to be changed.

Although many feminists now argue that women's equality can be gained only by enlisting the support of men, other feminists remain unconvinced. They remind the women's movement that male help in the past has often proved to be the thin end of a wedge of cooption and sabotage. They also stress the basic point that more power and responsibility for women inevitably leads to less power and responsibility for men. Is there any evidence, they ask, that men are willing to give up their privileges?

Although the contemporary women's movement has differed from its predecessor in its unwillingness to work with men, both movements found a similar stumbling block in the matter of social class. Members of the women's suffrage movement usually came from among the more leisured middle class. My own data on the second wave of twentieth-century feminists indicate that the same assumption cannot be made about activist members of this group. They came from families who were originally working class or lower middle class but who were upwardly mobile and had moved into middle-class status when these daughters were nearly adults. The women's identity as middle class was therefore largely on the basis of their achievements as adults. The fact remains, however, that the contemporary movement, like the earlier one, had considerable difficulty involving working-class women in large numbers. But during the 1970s, general consciousness increased about equal pay for equal work and about equal job opportunities; as clerical and factory workers organized themselves around these issues, working-class women became part of the women's movement.

Let us look more closely at some of the views, attitudes, and activities contained within the current women's movement. Perhaps the most striking thing is the movement's diversity. There is, of course, the central focus of agreement: women must work together to fight a common oppression. But within the movement are many different explanations for *why* women are universally subordinated and, accordingly, many different approaches to challenging that subordination.

Within the British women's movement, for example, there is a marked division between the views and political activities of two groups of activist women: socialist feminists and radical feminists. Socialist feminists see women's oppression in present-day society as a consequence of the workings of capitalism; their political priorities therefore lie in changing the ways in which the capitalist system has structured the division of labor between men and women. These women differ from traditional socialists in that they see sex oppression as a complex and important area that cannot wait for change until "after the revolution." Radical feminists, on the other hand, see male desire for power and control as a basic, universal fact of life, predating the capitalist economy. Women who hold this view regard any cooperation with men as totally counterproductive and concentrate their energies on developing women's culture and, insofar as possible, separate women's economies. Similar, and further, differences of approach can be seen in the women's movement in other European countries and in the United States.

The influence of the women's movement, however, has spread well beyond its core activists. Economic recession and a rising divorce rate in the Western world have led to the entry into the work world of many women who never expected to take on major economic responsibilities. The assumption of these responsibilities and the accompanying realization that female employees are treated less favorably than their male colleagues have served to raise the feminist consciousness of many women.

Large numbers of other women who would not previously have identified themselves as feminists have become involved in single-issue campaigns, such as a women's right of choice in the matter of abortion or the need for improved child-care facilities or campaigns for world peace. An involvement of this kind has often led to a general rethinking of the position of women in society and a reappraisal of the values underlying that society. Can it be right, many of these women ask, that government funding seems always to be available for weapons of destruction but rarely forthcoming for improving or even maintaining the standard of child care and education?

Throughout the Western world, and increasingly in the Third World, women are forming caucuses and groups within political parties, trade unions, and national and international organizations in order to press home the message that women — and women's values — can no longer be ignored. Although such efforts have had notable successes, the difficulties involved are tremendous. Paradox abounds in a world that now not infrequently gives lip service to women's rights but is still reluctant to make the basic changes required to usher in the era of women's equality. Personnel practices of UN administrative offices illustrate this point. Work at the UN — a body that purports to do much to promote women's equality — is divided into "general services" and "professional" jobs. The general service jobs are further divided between clerical jobs, which are "female," and maintenance jobs, which are "male" and pay at a higher rate. Eighty percent of general service jobs are occupied by women. In the professional ranks, which entail higher pay and more recognition, 80 percent of the jobs (including all the highest-level positions) are held by men.

Despite such continuing paradoxes, the Western women's movement has run into problems in its attempts to keep up a steady pressure on organizations and individuals that perpetrate injustices against women. In some ways, the success of the movement has impeded its progress. As we saw early in this book, a new generation of women now reaps the benefits of earlier struggles but does not recognize the importance of consolidating and extending achievements. These women do not really comprehend the struggle that was required to make their life style. It is immensely important that more young women come to a full understanding of the situation, for if a future of equality between the sexes is to be grasped, then these women must play an active part in bringing it within reach.

Feminism and Politics

In 1973 Betty Friedan commented to a gathering of feminists from all over the world that "feminism transcends politics." Sadly, the succeeding years have proven her wrong on this point. The progress of sex equity has many times fallen victim to the politics of parties nationally and the international arena.

The UN conferences on women in 1975 and 1980, for example, were characterized by the primacy of international power brokerage and bickering. At the Mid-Decade Conference held in 1980 at Copenhagen, the focus of attention lay not on worldwide progress toward women's equality (the ostensible subject of the conference) but on the question whether and how the UN organizations were to provide economic and moral support to the Palestine Liberation Organization (PLO) and the Southwest Africa Peoples Organization (SWAPO). As speeches and demonstrations continued into the second week of the conference, it became clear that in fact the real focus of attention did not even lie in these causes. The entire conference, like many UN functions, was simply another arena in which Western countries confronted Soviet bloc nations; while both blocs alternately wooed and reviled the Third World nations.

Several clear messages emerged from the proceedings of these conferences, however. Perhaps the most important is that men and male institutions are deeply threatened by the sight of women working together across national and international boundaries. Women's voices are to be heard only when they establish their credentials in the man-made establishment and according to the rules mandated by that establishment. Women are to be accepted as full citizens only when the men who invite them to join the club are fairly sure that they will pursue the same objectives as their male benefactors. Feminism by no means transcends politics.

It may be helpful at this point to look more closely at the sociopolitical conditions that are most likely to underline the development of a strong feminist movement. Three basic facts are of particular relevance.

1. Social movements by their very nature have social, political, and psychological components. These "particles" coalesce because an objective demands participation on all three levels. Usually, after the objective has been achieved, the movement disperses; some factions within it may even argue over particular differences.

2. Social and related political movements are more likely to emerge in a society that has a fairly high level of economic stability and security.

When life is a daily battle for survival, there is neither time nor energy for carefully planned social agitation.

3. Social movements gain momentum when the difference between the haves and have-nots is not so wide as to seem unbridgeable.

A moment's consideration of these facts can cast some light on the current women's movement. It is, for example, not surprising that the movement originated in North America and Western Europe; both places are characterized by a fair degree of political and economic stability. Neither is it surprising that the American women's movement first involved radical activist women and middle-class suburbanites frustrated with the feminine mystique. Or that on the Asian subcontinent and in Latin America the feminist initiative came from women of the upper classes, many of whom held government or professional positions.

Recognition of these facts may enable feminists to look ahead and plan for the future. Third World countries, for example, are increasingly likely to be the focus of feminist activity as the standard of living rises and as women in these countries have more access to education and communication and more control over their own bodies.

Who Wants "Superwoman"?

As the proportion of women in the workforce has increased throughout the world and as fresh career choices have become possible for women, a new specter has been presented to confront and confound them. This is the challenge of the "Superwoman," that elegant figure whose coolly competent smile never fades whether she is taking her baking out of the oven or removing important files from her executive briefcase. Effortlessly, Superwoman is in complete control of both her domestic and her work life. The only problem with Superwoman is that she does not exist.

Recognizing this, Betty Friedan and others have suggested that the problem for contemporary women in the Western world is no longer the frustration of "housewifery" but the frustration of women's desire for wifehood and motherhood in the face of demands from the workplace. But this is by no means the whole story, nor the version of the story most useful to "women in transition."

Increasingly, the economy of postindustrial societies has demanded a two-income rather than one-income family. The soaring cost of living has meant that comparatively few families can afford to rely on the sole earnings of one breadwinner. And the stabilization of population growth in the developed world has meant that the only way to increase the gross national product is to redistribute labor — and that necessarily involves persuading women to leave their homes for factories and offices. For both reasons, married women have been entering the workforce in large numbers whether or not their orientation is a "feminist" one.

What social patterns have evolved in socialist countries, where women make up an important part of the workforce? Women in Eastern Europe, particularly in the Soviet Union, have for generations faced the dual demands of the workplace and their domestic responsibilities. This has proved exhausting but possible because young children are cared for in state-run facilities and because women retire at an earlier age than men in order to pursue their *babushka* (grandmother) role. On collective farms in the Soviet Union, China, and Israel, household and "family" role responsibilities are incorporated into the productive economy. Even with these conditions, some women appear to be less than happy with the arrangements. For example, in Israeli kibbutzim there has been increasing clamor, by women and men, that they have their children with them at night and thus individualize child care.

In rural China, grandmothers retire at an earlier age than grandfathers in order to resume the traditional child-care and housekeeping function because communal child care has not fulfilled expectations. The allocation of domestic responsibilities is particularly difficult in China because both men and women who occupy professional positions are obliged to spend considerable time away from home each year. In some only partially industrialized societies — such as Ghana, Sri Lanka, and parts of Southeast Asia — women perform the major commercial function and also have the responsibility for caring for the children and the home.

Clearly, multiple role responsibilities are neither new nor extraordinary for many women in the world. Surely the important issue for the Western world is not to throw up collective hands in horror at the thought of impossible burdens descending on female citizens but, as in Scandinavia, to begin to develop social and economic facilities that share the burdens more equally between men and women. The intimidating figure of Superwoman is in reality a paper tiger, a woman of straw, the main purpose of which is to deter women from demanding full access to participation in the political and economic arenas.

Fortunately, this is not the whole story. For at least a decade, many men have made considerable efforts to respond to the challenges posed by feminism. Yet in the men's consciousness-raising groups that evolved from Farrell's work, *The Liberated Man,* the atmosphere was heavy with confusion and guilt.[5] It is currently fashionable to blame the women's movement for the masculine malaise, just as it used to be fashionable to blame "Super-moms" for men's inadequacies. With divorce statistics rising rapidly and single-parent families the norm in many places, the women's movement is now targeted as the culprit.

It is not feminism that is destroying the family, nor will feminism be the undermining force in the demise of traditional family values in decades to come. Feminism has not advocated that women enter the workforce in the same way as men have occupied it; feminism has not demanded that every family be supported by a pair of breadwinners. Feminism has argued and advocated a value system in which women's work and men's work would be identical, shared and valued depending on interests and talents as human beings. Instead, the past decade and portents of the future have been dominated by an economic condition that has required two breadwinners per family and has rewarded women only insofar as they have adopted the virtues and behaviors conventionally associated with successful men.

Superwoman is not "supermom." Rather, she is the female version of Superman. The latter was never a comfortable possibility. Feminism has never mandated such roles nor approved of them. Nontraditionalists who advocate androgynous roles have neither argued against the family nor argued in favor of one-parent families, two working parents with latchkey children, and women-skirted versions of the man in the gray flannel suit. An androgynous world would allow both parents scope to experience and express nurturant behaviors conventionally associated with "mothering," career patterns consistent with talents and temperaments, and cooperative or noncompetitive work schemes.

The prevailing economic system that requires the *competitive* labors of two adults in order to meet a decent standard of living for themselves and their children also detracts from the development of an intense sharing relationship between two adults that could evolve into a dynamic lifelong relationship.

Female Bonding

It is an interesting and seldom analyzed fact that there have been many more polygamous societies than polyandrous ones. Sometimes this has been attributed to the superior strength of the man contrasted with the "natural" dependency of the woman. Lionel Tiger used this fact to illustrate the "natural" proclivity of men for a full and varied sex life.[6] Desmond Morris rationalized this behavior through reference to the "harem" principle among other species with the male hunter providing for the needs of many and the females engrossed in the cycle of pregnancy and caring for the helpless young in a relatively protected environment.

I did not question these assumptions until one clear day while I was observing the sea lions' domestic dynamics on the islets off the California coast. I was watching intently and was shocked to discover that the particular "bull" I had been observing was in fact a cow. *She* was making the rounds from islet to islet, checking out the bulls and selecting one or another to tease into pursuit of her. Before the day was over, I realized that female sea lions socialized with one another, provoked males into a chase, and *selected* the males with whom they would engage in these games. So the female was the chooser, and among the females there was apparent camaraderie. Lionel Tiger, Desmond Morris, and their fellows were in error. Female animals bond together even to initiate mating games.

Women, whether in the harems of the Orient or involved with the struggle to turn wilderness into farms in nineteenth-century America, also worked together and shared with one another. Women's subordination is managed through the control and prevention of their bonding with other women.

There is no purpose served in dichotomizing women in terms of "feminists" versus "traditionalists," or in using mainstream political terminology that identifies women along national or geographic spectrums. Objectives for an individual or a group may differ depending on specific circumstances, but the goal of equal rights and opportunities has not been challenged by any women's group. Specific objectives – the passage of an Equal Rights Amendment, women's right to abortion, or "family allowances" – may differ, but regardless of their place in the spectrum of development, women value the integrity of their bodies and the equality of their contribution to the group.

Notes

1. Betty Friedan, *The Feminine Mystique* (New York: Dell, 1963).
2. Simone de Beauvoir, *The Second Sex* (New York: Knopf, 1949).
3. Betty Friedan, *The Second Stage* (New York: Summit, 1981).
4. C. Wright Mills, *The Sociological Imagination* (New York: Oxford University Press, 1959).
5. Warren Farrell, *The Liberated Man* (New York: Bantam, 1975).
6. Lionel Tiger, *Men in Groups* (New York: Random House, 1969).

Chapter **9**   THE FUTURE OF SEX ROLES

Several decades ago when I entered a classroom full of six-year-olds whose first educational experience was to be under my tutelage I realized with a jolt that I had a responsibility for the fulfillment of my generation and the creation of the next. I looked around and saw that the future is me! How many other women that year were feeling this sense of personal responsibility to create a very different world from that in which they had been molded?

For all of us who compare notes at international, intercultural, transdisciplinary, and interreligious conferences on women, there is always an element of surprise in the realization that the present is so very different from the future we envisaged for ourselves as adolescents. It is not that we lacked ambition or a drive for power but that we expected our choices to be fewer and our scope narrower. Whether we grew up in a world of men in gray flannel suits or where men wore sarongs, we anticipated the frustrations of our mothers as our own.

What Are Sex Roles?

In the course of this book I have discussed many ways in which Western society in particular transforms "male" and "female" into "masculine" and "feminine." This transformation lies at the heart of what is called sex-role stereotyping. "Sex roles" refer to the differential ways in which boys and girls, men and women, are supposed to take their places in the world; "stereotyping" indicates a process of ascribing characteristics that takes no account of the differences between individuals.

The new sex roles have imposed a new set of norms and expectations of what is "right," and men and women alike are afraid to be left behind. The masculine impotence researched and successfully treated by Masters and Johnson had psychological bases in sex-role norms that demanded passivity in women and initiative from men. Now men are suffering psychologically from the equally impossible demands of women.

Sometime in the 1970s the chartered course of the "new woman" took some ironic twists. While feminists were marching and shouting for the right to role equality and equal value for "women's work," most women's image of "success" remained the image of the successful male. The male power figure wanted and achieved a demanding job that required alienation from home, spouse, and children; he manfully plunged into competition so intense that it brought on high blood pressure and heart attacks and an excessive reliance on alcohol and cigarettes. He had to be assertive and aggressive. Although a generation of sociologists inveighed against the personal and social consequences of the gray-flannel-suit syndrome, many "liberated" women donned its feminine equivalent after reading *How to Dress for Success*[1] and took courses in assertiveness training.

In the first rush of good intentions, working women were suddenly selected by their male superiors to participate in various "upward bound" programs. A few were even singled out for big promotions. But in general, when the recruiting officers of large corporations reached out to find ambitious women to put into their management structures or boardrooms, could they find them? In many cases, no. Many women were unwilling to don male-type clothes and male aspirations. That was the first jolt to both male and female expectations. Many working women did not want to move up or out or anywhere. They liked where they were, and although they had not reached the limit of their abilities (or competence), they did not want to go any higher.

Jolt number two was that the few women who did move up and into decision-making positions of power turned out to be as ruthless and competitive with other women as men were with other men. Jolt number three was that their female subordinates often attempted to undermine them in ways they would not have tried with male superiors. And another jolt to the fair-minded intentions of both sexes in this bureaucratic stir-up was that those women who acquired power and who also happened to be more than moderately attractive were accused (by men and women) of having used their physical attributes to reach the top, the implication being that maleness and plainness are handicaps. A reversal indeed.

In the last decade there have been enormous changes in the sex-role expectancies of men and women both in the workplace and in the family, but it is only natural that the route from a sexist to an androgynous society should produce transitional obstacles and surprises. Accordingly, I propose to look at sex roles from the perspective of the transition generation and to speculate on the nature of the androgynous society toward which many women, and certainly many sensitive and fair-minded men, aspire.

The sex-role system is a complex and octopuslike phenomenon. Three factors can be identified as central to its operation. First, there is the assignment, on the basis of sex, of personality traits. In Western society, in the words of recent researchers, "dominance, aggression and objectivity have been associated with the male while passivity, tenderness and subjectivity have been associated with the female."[2] Second, there is the allocation, again on the basis of sex, of appropriate activities and work. We have already noted the disastrous economic implications of such allocation for women in the workforce. Third, there is the universal assumption that the male — or, by association, any attribute or activity considered "masculine" — is somehow intrinsically more valuable and important than the female or the "feminine."

These, then, are the bare bones of the system. They creak together to make up a formidable piece of social machinery, affecting every area of life. The lives and expectations of men and women are shaped and constrained by this system, but the roles ascribed to women tend more often to be the unsatisfactory walk-on parts.

The low proportion of women in scientific and technological careers provides a good example of how the sex-role system can work both to limit individual women's expectations and opportunities and to waste a nation's resources. The representation of women in science and engineering at all levels in Western society has shown a steady increase over the past two decades. But most women are still at the lowest levels, both in terms of academic achievement and employment. Fewer girls than boys take physical science courses in the first place; and they are less likely to persist with them.

Why are girls reluctant to prepare themselves for careers in science and technology? You may remember that in an earlier chapter we discussed — and exposed — the myth that girls are "naturally" inferior in this field. What we are left with, then, is a dismal story of lack of encouragement and support from the earliest years on. Parents praise the young boy who shows an interest in mechanical things. But they are less likely to express approval of his sister when she comes home with oily, dirty hands and clothes. At primary school, girls are rarely offered the opportunity to work at craft subjects such as technical drawing and woodwork. The result, as many teachers have testified, is that girls in secondary school lack confidence in their ability to tackle the practical experiments required in science class.

From the secondary school stage on, things get worse. Increasingly, girls learn to measure success in terms of social success; and social success usually depends on conforming to the feminine stereotype. It takes a singularly determined and self-confident adolescent girl to withstand ridicule from her peers and discouragement from her elders and persevere with studying what are still seen as "masculine" subjects. Interestingly, girls in single-sex schools are more likely to persevere with and gain qualifications in physical science subjects than girls in mixed schools. This finding suggests that the male domination of most mixed-schools results in narrower expectations of, and opportunities for, female pupils.[3]

At the university level, the proportion of girls studying scientific and technical subjects continues to fall. Nor does the story end here, in the educational establishment. Male scientists progress faster in their careers than their female colleagues.[4] The world of work reflects and reinforces the sex roles encouraged on the playground.

As the injustices of the sex-role system become more widely understood and as nations in economic recession begin to appreciate the value of the scientific talent currently being wasted, moves are being made to encourage girls to enter scientific and technical careers. In England, for example, the Engineering Industry Training Board has initiated a variety of schemes for recruiting girls and women to professional work in the industries it serves; and in the United States "affirmative action" programs attempt to increase the number of women working in these areas. However, until the sex-role system is challenged in its entirety — from the allocation of toys according to the sex of the child to the later allocation of domestic responsibilities — women are unlikely to be able to pursue their scientific and technological interests on the same footing as their male colleagues.

A sex-role system of one kind or another is deeply entrenched in most human societies, a fact that has given rise to a common argument that sex roles are in some way "natural," based on immutable biological facts. In earlier chapters we saw that evidence produced to show that female human beings have basically different needs and capacities from male human beings has been massively outweighed by evidence that the two sexes have many more similarities than differences. Here I would like to explore the implications of the fact that particular sex roles, unlike the biological roles of male and female in reproduction, are *not* universal. If different societies inculcate different sex roles, then the argument that such roles are based on universal biological facts is invalid. And anthropological evidence abounds that different societies expect different qualities — and attributes — from their men and women. In Western society today, men are expected to be competitive and aggressive, interested more in caring for themselves than other people; in other societies, women are the more "public" people, responsible for the economic support of their families. In Ghana, for example, women are in complete control of the distribution and retail of produce and use their economic autonomy to support and educate their children.

Attribution of sex-role expectations can, in itself, result in pathological and socially destructive behaviors. Social-psychological studies I conducted between 1963 and 1975 on adolescent pregnancy, drug abuse, and student evaluations of professors demonstrated the adverse consequences of such expectancies (see Appendix B).

A moment's reflection will show that history backs up the evidence of anthropology that sex roles are a product, not of nature, but of perceived social convenience. Without leaving the boundaries of Western societies, we can see that sex roles have changed markedly within a relatively short period of time. One writer has commented on women's roles in twentieth-century Britain:

> A woman born at the turn of the century could have lived through two periods when it was her normal duty to devote herself exclusively to her children; three when it was her duty to society to neglect them; two when it was right to be seductively "feminine," and three when it was a pressing social obligation to be the reverse; three separate periods in which she was a bad wife, mother and citizen for wanting to go out and earn her own living, and three others when she was an even worse wife, mother and citizen for not being eager to do so.[5]

A more detailed examination of the different lives and aspirations of two generations of twentieth-century women may give us a fuller idea of the various factors that can affect the definition of sex roles. Let us look, first, at the Western woman of the 1950s.

She probably belonged to a generation described by Betty Friedan as suffering from the "illness without a name."[6] She had been sold a bill of goods about motherhood, housewifery, consumerism, and washing machines that lasted through twelve children, a dog, and two cats! This woman was the antithesis of the enterprising and powerful New Woman envisaged by the feminists of the 1920s. And her individual withdrawal from the public arena was reproduced on a national scale: during the 1950s in the United States there were half as many women in higher education as there had been in the 1930s, and the number of women in professions (apart from elementary school teaching) had also fallen dramatically. The return of war veterans to college campuses had sparked a new competition among women for a title, *Mrs.*, rather than a degree. In droves they abandoned their university courses in favor of obtaining their PHT (Putting Husband Through).

But the roses round the door faded quickly. Women socialized into superfemininity found that their marriages did not provide a universe of satisfactions and that as their husbands moved up, they were left behind.

Divorce became more commonplace, and women had to start to think of themselves as providers of financial support as well as chief consumers. Conflicting feelings of fear, guilt, inadequacy, and ambition raged as women veered between emulating Wonder Woman and looking for a man's shoulder to cry on.

For the children of the 1950s — the daughters of those superfeminine women — things were different. They started learning the ways of being female at a time when rising affluence in Europe and America combined with the population explosion to exert pressure on women to reenter the labor force as nurses and teachers. The prospect of higher education opened up before these young women to a greater degree than ever before. As they grew up, they were likely, if American, to become involved in the civil rights movement and, if British, to become concerned about equal pay and anti-discrimination legislation. While the previous generation had started to question the validity of the sex-role system and had been caught in considerable psychological crossfire as a result, the women of the 1960s had fewer inner conflicts; they were already oriented to the idea of a society in which people were granted equal rights and liberties. In addition, the greater availability of contraception and abortion enhanced these women's sense of independence and autonomy. In many significant respects, their world was very different from that of their mothers.

New Is Not Always Better

Deeply rooted as they are in social mores and individual psychology, sex roles cannot be changed without considerable anguish and confusion. It is necessary, however, to remember that adapting to an inappropriate sex role also causes pain and frustration and that conventional Western sex roles are firmly based on women's economic and social oppression.

In *The Cinderella Complex*,[7] Colette Dowling considered the implications of the fact that the socialization of little girls reinforces dependency behaviors. She argued that this learned helplessness is a part of the psyche of the adult women; and it is a part that interferes with her achieving independence. For many women, she concluded, autonomy is as much feared as desired.

Having interviewed hundreds of women from many different cultures and social strata, I challenge these conclusions. Helplessness and dependency *are* learned behaviors, but just as significantly, they are the regressive reaction of a person (man or woman) who has been traumatized or victimized. Learned helplessness is something empire builders inflict on colonized peoples; they establish institutions that exclude the indigenous population from participation or status. Adult women striving for upward economic mobility and educational equality regress to helplessness when, having all the necessary qualifications, they are nonetheless rejected. They regress to helplessness when their personal integrity and self-respect are threatened by sexual harassment from male colleagues or supervisors. They regress to helplessness when they are made to feel guilty about their focus on work rather than the family. The vital point is that helplessness can be unlearned as well as learned; it is not a burden that every adult woman must continue to carry.

Sex roles have rarely changed as rapidly as they have in the West during the last twenty years. It is hardly surprising, therefore, that individual and social uncertainty and confusion have conspired to create some new stereotypes that are potentially as crippling as the old sex roles.

The sexual liberation movement that ran its course during the same decades as the other rights movements so effectively destigmatized premarital and extramarital sex that many young women were pressured into promiscuity. It would seem clear that "getting in touch" with oneself sexually should mean that one could choose *not* to become sexually involved just as freely as one could opt for sexual involvement. Nevertheless, many younger women became heir to the same anxiety that haunted men for years: orgasmic competence.

Becoming a Feminist

It seems a lifetime ago that I was confronting the problem of getting into a graduate program in psychology. Having dropped out of graduate school once to support my husband through his doctorate and having a few babies on the way, I was applying to university programs in a new location and from a new role predicament. I was doing some work as a consultant using psychological tests and techniques and had also remained actively involved in teaching young children in public and private schools. As I made up a *curriculum vite* for my applications, I realized that there was a brief period of time not covered by paid work experience, and I hoped I wouldn't be asked about that. I also knew that it was harder for a married woman to gain acceptance into graduate school and so on the application form, where it said *marital status,* I wrote "not applicable."

My credentials carried me through the first stage of application; then came a face-to-face interview with the chairman of the department. Prior to leaving the house, I removed my wedding band and carefully checked to assure that there was no evidence of any of the three babies on my person. The interview went well until the chairman picked up my vita and, scrutinizing it carefully, said, "And what were you doing between 1958 and 1960?" I wasn't prepared for this and, blushing, sputtered something about "having babies. . . ." He looked at me and said, "But you aren't married?" I answered, "That's right." I left the interview feeling that it was somehow less damaging to my chances to be thought an unmarried mother than a married one.

I finally got back into a doctoral program but not without being told by prominent psychologists who headed departments in California, Illinois, Michigan, and Wisconsin, "We have very few places in our clinical program, and we want to give these to candidates who are not only clearly superior students — you have demonstrated that you are one of them — but, more important, to people who will use their education for many more years. Women do not use their training — they get married and have children and stay at home supported by their husbands." In short, their attitude was that women need Mrs. before their name rather than Ph.D. after it.

My experience was not an isolated one. Some years later, when the Association for Women in Psychology presented the facts to the board of directors of the American Psychological Association, I was one of the group that informed this august body that on the then available statistics, women in psychology averaged longer careers in the profession than men. Then and later, we communicated many other "awkward" pieces of information to the psychology profession about psychologists.

By then I had achieved my credentials in sociology and published a good deal in political science as well. My confrontations with directors of professional associations continued, however, and they left me with many new questions. Given the difficulty of acceptance into graduate programs and the problems of clawing their way toward occupations, what kinds of women were becoming professionals? What life experiences and social circumstances combined to make a woman a psychologist, physician, architect, or lawyer? Moreover, why were some women feminists, while others remained traditionalists?

To find answers to these questions I devised a detailed questionnaire (it appears as Appendix A at the end of this book) and posted it to 100 women psychologists; a number of colleagues compiled a similar list of questions for interviewing women physicians and architects. We learned a great deal. One of the most remarkable pieces of new information that emerged from the original study was that not one of the 100 women psychologists believed she was functioning in the role she had envisaged for herself when she was sixteen. The same was generally true of the physicians and architects. Most of these women had expected *either* a career *or* marriage and family, or some chronological separation of the two (career first and family afterward, or vice versa), or at most a part-time career involvement while bringing up a family. Yet those psychologists who had married had full-time careers *and* full-time family responsibilities and were often single parents to boot. The physicians, by and large, had envisaged full-time careers — they had not considered marriage and family — yet most had acquired families as well as full-time careers. In contrast to the psychologists, the majority of these women had not entertained the possibility of a career first and marriage afterward. They had their sights set on a full-time, lifelong career in medicine.

Interestingly, the responses of the 100 psychologists who answered the questionnaire fully showed that few of them had originally intended to make a career in psychology; most had been ambitious to enter careers in more characteristically male-dominated professions but had been discouraged from pursuing them for that reason. Significantly, most of them felt that they were not pursuing the life style that their fathers, husbands, or men in general would have chosen for them, and that their mothers would not have particularly approved either. Yet the majority placed a fairly high value on their intellectual abilities, precisely the abilities they thought their fathers most valued in them. This same group was also of the opinion that their parents exhibited fewer sex-role polar differences (were more androgynous) than other parents of their day. Significantly, almost all the younger women had completed their graduate work before the age of thirty and reported less dissuasion from others in their choice of a career in psychology.

All the women in this original study were women in transition, and at the time (1972) they were not all feminists. Many felt little kinship with the nascent women's movement, and less than half considered their problems to be related to the conflicting roles of career and motherhood.

Another question raised by studies of women professionals that had significance for the future of women was how women redefine their roles. The women professionals had, for the most part, accepted the role restrictions extant in their childhood. When choosing a masculine profession, they had either forfeited their biological role in procreation and their social role in marriage or had switched their aspirations toward other professions or vocations in which their femininity would be less in conflict with their work. Instead of presenting a new role model, these women bought into one of the older ones. Jessie Bernard[8] points out that medieval abbesses and the nuns who surrounded them were released from family responsibilities by their vows and therefore were free to exercise their skills and talents. As it turned out, they exercised these very much as men did. There were two rival claimants to become abbess of Poitiers; the loser collected a band of fighters, attacked the nunnery, and was routed only by sheer force of arms. Bernard relates this incident to the early stages of the renewed feminist movement in the 1960s when women, to make their point, broke the norms of female behavior and expressed their rage verbally and with physical aggression. Women who forsake procreation in favor of the workplace, and women who express their freedom from sex-role stereotypes by enacting mirror-image behaviors, are hardly representative of an innovative and androgynous system.

My follow-up research on the lives and concerns of professional women not only reinforced some of the implications of my earlier work but also raised new questions and issues. Some of these women had never married; others had experienced a significantly greater than average rate of marital breakdown. The women psychologists who reported themselves happily married were married to men who were also psychologists or in a closely allied profession (medicine and the law predominated). Most of the younger women had married *after* completing their professional training. No one in these samples was married to a man in a semiskilled or unskilled occupation. These women were liberated from the traditional taboos that excluded their sex from the professions, but their social status was still partly a consequence of their relationships with men, fathers, husbands, and colleagues. To what extent, I wondered, does social status influence a woman's or a man's attitudes toward success and toward feminism?

In an attempt to answer this question I studied a number of women who regarded themselves as feminists and a number who did not. Working women who are not feminists tend to have husbands in blue-collar or clerical occupations, seldom among the higher echelons. Both working and nonworking women who are feminists tend to have husbands who are upwardly mobile; the women themselves aspire to their husbands' positions or higher. Feminists in 1972 and 1974 were a narrower sample of women then they were in 1981. Many of them, like Betty Friedan, put themselves in the occupational category of "housewife." Ironically, many of the nonfeminist working women included in our 1975 study also gave their occupation as "housewife." Their reasons for working were different from the reasons given by feminists: nonfeminists worked because they needed the income to supplement their husbands' earnings or because they were the sole support for themselves or a family; they had little interest in advancement or in improving their skills, or if they did, they had done little or nothing about it. Feminist women, on the other hand, whether they were in the workforce or not, had specific plans for achieving specific goals. Sometimes these goals were presented in a very detailed fashion.

In the early 1970s there were differences in family background and therefore in childhood experiences and conditioning between women who were feminists and women who were traditionalists. By the end of the decade, a generation of young adult women had entered the workforce whose educational experience had been more egalitarian regardless of family origin. They were unused to viewing themselves as "the second sex" in the distribution of wages, benefits, and promotions. While these younger women might not identify themselves as feminists, they were also unlikely to define their social standing by reference to their spouses or to select a spouse on the basis of social standing.

Some of the social and psychological characteristics of the minority of women who became feminists in the 1960s and early 1970s were much more commonplace in the generation that succeeded them (and are likely to become even more so in the future). Among these characteristics was a family background of a wife's place in the workforce with a husband who was supportive about the kind of work she did. Often husband and wife were of different religions and sometimes of different races; both husband and wife were achievement-oriented. Nor was it unusual for the wife to be more highly educated than the husband.

Feminists of the 1960s tended to have been born into families that had moved at least one notch up the socioeconomic scale by the time their daughters were sixteen. Those feminists who had children had fewer children than their parents. As individuals, these women were gregarious, sophisticated, good at organizing themselves and others, decisive, and eager to achieve.

There were some differences between European and American feminists in the early days of the feminist renaissance. European feminists tended to be of middle- or upper-class origin and o have worked in higher-status jobs; the reverse was generally true of American feminists. Women in countries usually considered less advanced, such as Mexico and India, tended to achieve higher positions in government than did Europeans and North American women. In these countries, too, legislation favoring women arrived somewhat earlier than it did in Europe and North America. In Mexico and India, however, it must be remembered that upper-class women enjoyed privileged political status. While they had access to educational and economic opportunities and power, their lower-class sisters were, as James Connolly once described Irish women, "slaves of slaves."[9]

The fact that the dichotomy between sex roles is greatest in groups with the fewest resources has a hopeful implication for the future of women: as the gaps narrow between the rich and poor, so will the differences between sex roles and socialization.

The New Women and the New Man

Any fundamental change in sex roles will entail considerable rethinking of individual and social attitudes. It will also necessitate a substantial alteration of social and economic structures and institutions. At the moment, most of the structures of society still militate against women who wish to develop their potential. For example, even if a women is confident enough to know that she wants to be an engineer, and has persevered long enough to gain the necessary qualifications, the lack of good child-care facilities is likely to prevent her from pursuing her chosen career on an equal footing with similarly qualified men.

Even in relatively enlightened communities today there are, and will be, workplaces and work systems predicated on the idea that the worker is a man and that his family responsibilities give him pride of place in the economic reward system. Yet the woman who recognizes her family responsibilities is penalized by the work institution − she loses promotions, seniority, and wages by leaving the workforce in order to bear and care for children. Part-time jobs are either dead-end or nonexistent in fields that offer satisfying and lucrative careers. Moreover, part-time work carries no fringe benefits and is usually paid by the hour. In full-time careers there is often the problem that differences in sex-role socialization mean that a woman is likely to handle a particular job differently from a man and so be judged as "ineffective" when she is merely "different."

The role of mother/wife is universally mandated to take priority for women. Societies consider child care and housework to be the duty of society at large only when the mother (not the father) is viewed as unfit for the job either by reason of poverty or moral deficiency or both. It hardly needs to be said that the operation of these sex roles is reflected in the existence of "women's work" and in fact that women's salaries continue to be so much lower then men's

Generational differences in the sex-role socialization of American women are apparent in the responses to my biodemographic questionnaire from American women born in the 1920s, 1930s, 1940s, 1950s, and 1960s, (reprinted in Appendix A).

As we have seen, restrictive sex-role stereotypes operate in the public and private spheres, hampering the efforts of both men and women to live broad and full lives. Change is bound to be difficult and complicated; there is no reason to expect that sex-role stereotyping can be eradicated in one or even two generations. On the individual level it is not surprising that transitional women — and transitional men — experience considerable confusion and dissonance. Let me give you two examples.

Deirdre is a twenty-four-year-old client of mine. A divorced woman, she is intelligent, mechanically talented, and chronically depressed. She introduced one session by asking the question, "Do you believe in premenstrual tension?" She had been suffering increasingly from mood swings and had begun to relate them to her menstrual cycle. Now, when one is ill or aching, one is only too likely to feel low in spirits, and cycle changes indeed cause ups and downs in temperament for both women and men. But in Deirdre's case there is more to her depression than PMT; indeed, she is something of a psychological paradox at the moment.

She has been reinforced by her parents into dependency, is afraid of independence, but is passively aggressive against her parents' decisions for her "well-being." She wants love, craves physical affection, and feels that she cannot succeed at anything except being a good wife for an upwardly mobile man. But she also wants to achieve something in her own right. For years she has listened to the engineers she dates and has wanted to do similar work. She has good potential for engineering or mechanical education, and yet she is afraid of mathematics.

Deirdre is not a child of the liberation movement, although her childhood years spanned its flowering. Her parents are affluent, professional, and urbane. Deirdre's father told his daughters, "You should go to a good university because there you will find the right kind of husband." The daughters had lessons in the arts and went to summer camps. If anyone wants to talk about the influence of the Peloponnesian War on Greek sculpture, Deirdre is terrific! She also knows how to entertain and could push a husband through the executive ranks. Deirdre's parents directed her to "be happy." Neither they nor she can understand why she is depressed.

Another client, Jim, suffered from crippling anxieties associated with sex-role expectations. A successful economist in the U.S. Civil Service, he was finding it increasingly difficult to concentrate on his job and produce work of high quality. He also had an uneasy relationship with his father and was experiencing sexual problems with his girl friend. The focus of much of his difficulty seemed to be a conflict between the work he was engaged in and his political ideals. A political radical, he strongly disapproved of the free enterprise system that his work was bolstering.

As therapy progressed, a recurrent theme identified the difficulty he was experiencing in meeting the expectations he believed other people had of him. His job was consistent with what he thought others required of him and was a kind of token identification with "the system." But the course of his career was running counter to his personal and political desires and beliefs; he was trapped by the masculine stereotype. It became clear that what at first seemed a work-related problem, or possibly an unresolved oedipal problem, was actually a conflict between sex-role expectations and personal desires.

Eventually, Jim decided that his personal desires were more important than the expectations of others, and he changed his job to one that afforded him no similar conflict. On a personal level he became much more open about his thoughts and feelings, and he found that a considerable burden had been lifted from his shoulders. Feminist therapy, he agreed, had helped him enormously.

Of course, feminist therapy or any therapy not oriented to adjustment to traditional normative goals did not exist in the 1950s and 1960s. When I was on the faculty of a major university, widely known for its graduate programs in psychology, in 1973, the director of the university's psychological services clinic told me that it was sufficient for the needs of women clients, including lesbians, that a woman was on the treatment staff. He claimed, moreover, that role modeling was the only reason that the clinic employed any women at all. During the previous year, the American Psychological Association Task Force on Women in Psychology had issued a report that supported the value of feminist therapy and sharply criticized the reinforcing of sex-role stereotypes and institutional programs that assessed mental health in stereotypical terms. The news had not yet reached that clinic director. In the decade since then, the news has traveled; it is no longer considered irrelevant or bizarre. In psychotherapy and in vocational counseling, there is less effort to connect a person's psyche to an expected role.

Dissonance between person and role and between achievement and ascribed status leads to serious psychic consequences. In earlier generations these conflicts and their behavioral manifestations formed a vicious circle known often as "women's problems" or "female personality." That women suffered more than men from sex-role-induced frustrations led to a false belief that there was a biological basis for such problems.

Feminist therapy offers a new way of resolving sex-role conflicts. The focus of treatment is the analysis and identification of these conflicts, and the goals of treatment are the replacement of maladaptive or self-destructive behaviors with constructive ones. The therapist's philosophy is that being female is consistent with being human and is no more constrictive nor role-defined than that.

If sex roles are abolished, will this lead to an androgynous society? Let us project from current scientific data the trends that may eventuate in the twenty-first century.

If men and women are not defined and limited in their range of choices by virtue of the XY distributions of chromosomes, then each life will confront a wide range of choices. This will be unlikely to take the "fun" out of heterosexual relationships, nor will it mandate a unisex appearance. Rather, each individual and each relationship between people will proceed in and through role behaviors that are not contingent on stereotyped expectations. No one will ascribe meaning or behaviors to others on the basis of gender alone. An intelligent and highly ambitious woman who wants to be a good wife and mother will not be deterred in choosing her life course. The man who is essentially gentle and paternal will find himself socially acceptable as a house-husband if that is his choice. Masculine potency and feminine sex appeal will no longer be anxiety-producing for adolescents and adults who are different from the images projected on billboards and TV screens. The anxiety that previously instigated destructive adolescent behaviors will not emanate from the differences the individual estimates between self and popular images (see Appendix B).

We are already adapting ourselves to this reality. The muscular specimen who used to feature prominently in fantasies of manhood and in films has been more often relegated to performing in comedies. Existing systems of organization and production that are competitive, hierarchical, impersonal, and too often alienating are already becoming archaic and counterproductive. As each society requires more productivity from each individual and as the nature of work changes, women's participation no longer has to be an underclass to exploit.

In order to change the world, the women's revolution, which has been called the only real revolutionary movement in the twentieth century, must move forward to fulfill its revolutionary definition. Forms and processes of organization and production must be constructed that are consistent with a feminist ideology that values centrifugal rather than hierarchical relationships and views humankind as capable of freedom.

Greater freedom entails greater responsibility, and as women gain their autonomy, they must address, in their own terms, the major issues facing the world. There are signs that this is happening. Women are in the forefront of campaigns for world peace. And when economic pressures are lifted and women are free to live their own lives, they have no hesitation in deliberately limiting the size of their families. In addition, women are centrally concerned about the quality and nature of the care and education provided to their children.

Yet it is unlikely that men and male institutions will be free of sexism and its consequences in the social, economic, and political spheres until women, as a class and individually, break through the vicious circle of prejudice. It is no easy task after extensive and repeated victimization to fight back against the victimizers, but this is the immense challenge facing today's women. Feminist therapy can help individual women to reassemble their forces and confidence. In the social and political spheres, bonding together with other women can provide the communal strength for action.

Notes

1. Rosabeth Moss Kantor, *Women and Men of the Corporation* (New York: Basic Books, 1977).
2. *The Times* (London), 14 August 1980.
3. Ibid.
4. Ruth Adam, *A Woman's Place: 1910-1975* (New York: Norton, 1975).
5. Colette Dowling, *The Cinderella Complex* (Garden City, N.Y.: Doubleday, 1980).
6. Jessie Bernard, *The Female World* (New York: Macmillan 1981).
7. Dowling, *Cinderella Complex.*
8. Bernard, *Female World.*
9. James Connolly, *The Re-conquest of Ireland* (Dublin: New Books, 1974).

Chapter **10** THE FUTURE *IS* WOMAN

There is neither a human nor a technological reason to expect that in the future women will retreat to their past status. There is every reason to believe that the next century will be the century of woman. During that century it is also conceivable that women's prominence will change the system's institutions and the system itself to fulfill the revolutionary potential of the women's movement.

It is ironic that women are taking their place in the labor force at precisely the same time that force is shrinking in postindustrial countries. Unemployment and recession discourage employers from investing in new workers and discourage workers whose career patterns are disrupted from risking new vocational programs. Yet even in times of economic discouragement, the economy is changing rapidly in terms of the occupations coming into existence as industries gear up by increasing automation and shrink to displace semiskilled workers.

There are new demands for engineers and computer programmers, and for others trained in such specialized areas as genetic engineering and design and the management of automated systems. The people who will install and operate the new sophisticated equipment must be trained and interested in their work.

But success breeds competition. In Norway, for instance, the very laws that have mandated preferential hiring of women in occupations from which they have been absent have become vehicles for admitting men into the top levels of traditionally female jobs that have become technologized and highly paid. For example, men seeking nontraditional careers are becoming surgical and intensive-care nurses. Since few of them are in the higher echelons of nursing, they must, according to equal opportunities laws in Scandinavian countries, be given preference in hiring. This might not be so troublesome if women were obtaining the requisite skills, training, and experience to enter the upper echelons of academe, for instance.

Unfortunately, most of the top-level positions in economic and political life are not only competitive but also require lengthy experience, which, at this time in history, women do not have, either because of discrimination against them in entry-level positions or because the demands of daily life have diminished their opportunities for obtaining the requisite experience for advancement.

In America, women's colleges came into being because the existing universities would not accept women. The Ivy League "sisters" flourished, but recently, as mergers occurred between major male and female colleges, the women's colleges lost their names and with them their identities. The women enrolled lost their last opportunity for an academic atmosphere that was essentially feminist. Ellen Goodman commented on the new arrangement between two of the famous paired institutions, Barnard (a women's college) and Columbia University. When Columbia offered a limited arrangement, Barnard turned it down because it was not a full partnership. Instead, as the *Washington Post* reported, "Young women applicants can choose between the female institution of Barnard, separate but dedicated to equality, and the male institution of Columbia, integrated but not yet equal. Somehow or other their choices seem familiar."[1]

The Direction of the Future

Several recognizable trends appear in the last quarter of the twentieth century that are portentous for the next century.

1. Increasingly high technology may standardize and upgrade human mental processes.
2. An increased need for service workers in the more advanced professions may technologize and render more complex the formerly mid-level occupations of nurse and teacher.
3. Changes are occurring in patterns of household occupancy and maintenance. For example, condo/collective cleaning and feeding systems may totally change housekeeping functions.
4. A need for increased per-capita productivity levels worldwide may produce new child-care arrangements that facilitate every adult's maximal participation in the workforce.

Some idea of the future can be seen dramatically through the space programs. What will people accomplish when they go to Mars? What will they do when they travel to another galaxy? They will use their brains and the superbrains we call computers to investigate, track, and predict things in the universe. Will they need a high level of testosterone to do this? Will they need beards to see the stars? Will they need to bend steel with their bare hands? I doubt it.

There is little reason to believe that space persons need to be men. Women have been piloting aircraft about as long as men have, and women have worked as test pilots and navigators for well over sixty years, but women were not among the initial personnel chosen for the space training program. There are women in that program now. And that is a good sign. In the twenty-first century the important tasks, the status positions, and the decision making must be performed by people regardless of gender.

The Workplace of the Future

Because it was through the economic life of the society that women were subjugated, it is through women's activity in the workplace that equality is a foreseeable reality. This is happening through the fortunate coincidence of two convergent trends. First, women's participation in the workforce is now necessary, and it establishes a new value for women and a new social status. Second, the nature of valued work has changed, including the style in which it is best accomplished and the physical requirements for performing the work. Moreover, the qualities that have successfully launched women into the workforce are not necessarily those of pseudo men, even in jobs that are physically demanding. Work in mines and on heights, for example, may be performed more effectively by a person who is smaller and lighter in weight.

Whether the workplace is a skyscraper office complex or a rural area in an underdeveloped country, technology has changed the nature of work and societies by a new demand for skilled labor pools. These changes, which are so interlocked that the world economy rises and falls in unison, portend enormous differences not only in the increased number of women in the paid workforce but also where they will work and how that work will be accomplished.

Technology may even permit members of the same office team to work together at great distances from one another. A secretary, operating a word processor in his or her home, may send out completed correspondence for signature and then have it transmitted for distribution. Boss and secretary may meet face-to-face once a week or less. Conferences via telephone lines may substitute for in-person staff meetings. Such arrangements, some of which are already in effect, will facilitate parental child-care planning.

Technological and industrial advances brought masses of people from the agrarian sections of the economy as improved farming methods lessened the need for farmers. More recently, migrant workers have come into the postindustrial countries of North America and Europe. Some women were uprooted in these moves, and others remained on subsistence farms with the elderly and the very young. Their work, gruelling and constant, has rarely been included in the index of the paid economy. The commercialization of agriculture, which follows on the technologization of farming, will be an additional social push away from peasant farming. It will require the transformation of subsistence activities into income-producing activities, and in raising the productivity of rural labor, will create new employment opportunities for women within and outside of agriculture.

For generations, the women of rural Portugal joked bitterly, "Oh, Maria got married because she wanted to be alone." Young husbands went off to the factories of France, and during their annual visits home, started another child to be born in their absence and raised as the mother's responsibility, along with her farming efforts. Now, Maria often goes with her husband; and in France, Germany, and the Scandinavian countries she may attend classes in literacy and language. Her children go to school and grow up knowing both parents, giving the man a share in providing nurturance and seeing the delight that children provide for parents.

In Tanzania, the government systematically, through the national women's organization, provides the means for the upward mobility of rural women, and through various projects to upgrade the economic production of the countryside, encourages men to remain on the land instead of migrating to the cities. By increasing the material and social resources within rural areas, as well as reducing inequities in access to these sources between rural and urban sectors, women have become active agents and beneficiaries of the development process. And men become less constrained by the macho symbols of the distant hunt and more free to express compassion, tenderness, and patience, the children will learn firsthand about an androgynous society.

Such programs do not have to be communicated formally to spread. They proliferate, probably by trial and error, as early humankind spread to the far reaches of Africa, Europe, and Asia.

During the United Nations Decade for Women, the UN Voluntary Fund provided the basis for projects in nine of the poorest countries that resulted in income-generating projects. This fiscal base, in turn, provided political clout for women within the family, the community, and the larger society.[2] While the interest of women was frequently overlooked in planning development priorities, the UN official emphasis on equalizing women's status provided the impetus as well as the financial resources to this end.

In postindustrial societies, as far as white-collar jobs are concerned, traditional women's skills are being newly valued. Increasing automation in industry and public service means that there is a new demand for highly developed clerical skills. Computers and word processors require the same expertise that has for a long time organized offices and operated typewriters and sewing machines. There is heartening evidence, too, that women are increasingly moving into designing, installing, and maintaining, as well as operating, the new equipment.

Other traditional female skills are also in new demand. Teaching, law, medicine, social services, and communication now openly acknowledge a need for practitioners who, on top of intellectual stamina, possess skills in nurturance, verbal fluency, and skills in interpersonal relationships. For a long time, these professions were dominated by a "scientific generation" — by men who were detached, distanced, and solitary. As we saw in an earlier chapter, American clinical psychology actively discriminated against graduate students who were sensitive or responsive to others. This "scientific generation" stood in sharp contrast with practitioners from their grandparents' time, who had been friends and neighbors.

Condominium apartment buildings, individually owned apartments that provide for homeownership while eliminating the responsibility for personal care and upkeep of the exterior structure, appear as the epitome of postindustrial private enterprise. In fact, the social dynamics of community technology are identical to the rural village in the less developed society, although the interpersonal relationships are considerably less focused.

Much as the condominium is a housing "commune," albeit a more materially enhanced one than a monastery, a Soviet collective, or a kibbutz, restaurants, including fast-food outlets, have become the communal dining rooms of postindustrial cities. Even when economies dwindle, an increasingly larger share of the food budget is spent dining out. The very nature of housework is shifting to the technological, specialist, marketplace process. The irony of our small world is that while those in the socialist world, including Polish workers and members of Chinese farm communes, move toward individual and nuclear family responsibilities as an alternative to state con.rol and communal priorities, the American and British bourgeoisie are developing a communism of the private sector in order to fulfill individual goals and career destinies.

Philosopher Robert Ingersoll once said there will never be a generation of great men until there has been a generation of free women. We have reached a historic watershed when only one-fifth of a woman's life need be devoted to childbearing and child rearing, *if she chooses to have children.* The life expectancy for women in postindustrial societies means that by the time a woman's children are spending most of their time in school, she will have more than half her life ahead of her. By the time her children leave home, she will have the number of years ahead of her that constituted the whole life expectancy for women two hundred years ago. If she remains married, she will live a tenth of her life as a widow. If she divorced, she will live alone when her children leave home. These facts led one futurist to predict that "whatever women resolve about dealing with careers, leisure, retirement and old age will set the pace for men, and will determine whether we are to enter upon a good society or one degraded by boredom and frustration."[3]

Breaking the Circle

The strategy for changing women and all human relationships starts with the recognition of oneself in context: knowing thyself. Self as woman is known through her past as daughter and through her mother as woman. Action for women begins with the *identity of sisterhood*. Unlike racial prejudice, which is alleviated by the "brotherhood" of white, black, and brown together, sexism is alleviated by a recognition of their common cause by women in "sisterhood."

Women must break through the barriers of sex-stereotyped jobs by considering the realities of the coming world. The technology that once alienated women has now put women on an equal footing for prospects in the world of work. The coming occupations for economic advantage are adaptations of what has been "women's work." Data processing, including programming, systems analysis, and database management; engineering, electronics, and energy; accounting and finance specialties; human resources; health and therapy; economics; marketing and sales — they are merely modern extensions of clerical jobs, retail salesclerking, household management, and making clothes or meals.

In the marriage marketplace of the future, another traditional principle has to be reworked. The woman's value in service to her family through her labor and wisdom once may have placed her far above rubies, but actually it assured her only of a roof over her head and the wherewithal to keep herself alive. Now the skills, training, and job prospects of a woman have become an attractive consideration for men in determining their future prospects together. The question is no longer "Can she cook and sew?" but "Do our life styles complement each other? Can we share our fiscal and social futures?"

Whereas women used to take their social identity from their marriage partners, men are now often in that situation by attending conferences of their wives' professional groups as "spouses" or, in the larger community, when the woman of the pair is a Supreme Court justice or member of Congress.

Two-income families have become the norm. Childless marriages are gaining acceptance. The identity of a couple based on the woman's occupation or fame is no longer unusual. There are some apparent setbacks to progress in the downward spiral of the world economy and in rising unemployment figures. And women's unemployment is higher than men's, for women are the last hired and first fired in most circumstances. And women are still seriously underrepresented in top echelons of institutions in which they overflow the lower strata. The future is designed for women's equality, however, and the present unfavorable conditions are likely to sound the death knell for a system that excluded women.

Increasingly, women from all strata and segments of society have recognized their common struggle, albeit with little ideological consistency articulated among them. But their varied backgrounds and circumstances have made a difference in the nature and directions taken by women, whether through the women's movement as such or in the mainstream of economic and political life. This is a positive portent for the future of women insofar as more women in more places are expecting and demanding and recognizing their common struggle for equality. What is unclear is whether this diversity of experience and focus will dictate tactics and strategies that are less effective, or even inconsistent, with feminist objectives. In terms of political strategy, this also suggests that in the United States there was insufficient mobilization of existing human resources toward ratification of the Equal Rights Amendment. Human resources in terms of consciousness-raised women are available, and must be mobilized for future change.

The goals of productive efficiency and capital accumulation, as they are at present pursued in Western society, mediate against the development of societies in which men and women can live out their full human potential. Any feminist ideology must challenge systems of production and organization.

As traditional social barriers are demolished, homosexual relationships will become more open and more accepted; people will be prepared for a life of multiple relationships rather than a lifetime's monogamy; and the social and legal stigmas surrounding children born out of wedlock will be removed. It seems likely that the link between monogamous heterosexual relationships and the rearing of children will be broken in other ways too. In several countries now, single parents and homosexual couples are allowed to adopt children; and many lesbian couples have acquired children through AID (artificial insemination by donor).

Another likely development is that less social significance will be attached to the relative ages of male and female sexual partners; no longer will it be considered appropriate for an older man to enter into a relationship with a much younger woman but inappropriate for an older woman to have a sexual relationship with a young man. The well-known anthropologist Margaret Mead described several societies in which a young man makes a first marriage with a considerably older woman and then a second marriage with a younger woman who will bear him children. The advantage of this system is that no one is ever initiated into sexuality by an inexperienced partner.[4] Societies of the future may incorporate similar patterns of behavior.

The demolition of traditional sex roles is likely to have another important effect, one of considerable personal significance to many people, both men and women. As social and personal identity become less bound up with gender and sexual identity, there may well be less social pressure on individuals to take part in unwanted, but expected, sexual activity.

In the vital area of child care, it is slowly being acknowledged that flexible arrangements are a requirement in order to satisfy both the child's and the parents' needs. Flexible working arrangements and flexible child-care groups and nurseries are increasingly being developed to meet economic realities and to share out the work — and the pleasure — associated with the care of children. It seems likely that housework and child care will become shared responsibilities not primarily because of prenuptial contracts or a commitment to women's equality but because technology and economic conditions are changing the nature of housework and child rearing.

The Future *Is* Now

Several years ago, in a speech at Harvard University, Bella Abzug said, "It isn't that I think women are superior to men, it's just that they haven't had the opportunity to be corrupted by power. We'd like that opportunity." With that statement Abzug identified a dilemma of the women's movement. Has the objective of the movement been to put women into boardrooms to make decisions that exploit others, just as men have done? Or is it possible to have a social change that will make women's culture an equal, alternative value system in a society that does not predicate achievement on sex-role stereotypes? This dilemma incorporates the problems of strategies and ideologies, cultural roots and changing role opportunities.

During the past decade, the Equal Rights Amendment to the Constitution has been defeated; Supreme Court decisions have reinforced discrimination in employment rights; and abortion clinics and family planning offices have been bombed. Most ominously, an anti-women's movement has been mounted and led by women who identify themselves as pro-life and pro-family. So styled, these antagonists of feminism have usurped the traditions of women's culture.

Despite these setbacks, some would argue that women today have it better than ever because the women's movement has become so integral to America. There are now two women in the Cabinet, a woman Supreme Court justice, and a woman vice-presidential candidate. Yet those who doubt that women still face a crisis in equity need only contemplate the implications of President Reagan's reiterated emphasis on the inviolability of the family in American society, or the executive order withdrawing U.S. financial support for programs that provide Third World women with abortions. Or consider those ads that say, "I think I'll keep her," or that glamorize sado-masochism with a man spanking a woman, or the current fad that features little girls as sex objects. These are potent signals that the objectives of the women's movement continue in obscurity on the American scene, that women are losing their impact as a movement. Where women once threatened disruption to big business and established interests, they have become somewhat more affluent consumers of the image the conventional powers currently dictate.

A few years ago, women went around depressed, and Betty Friedan articulated their grievances with suburbia. Now, women are trying to be bionic in order to prove themselves good wives and mothers, on the one hand, and top executives on the other.

The women's movement started its current round as a collective enterprise including women with widely differing ideologies or none at all. What they had in common was the conviction that women were getting a bum deal because their position and participation in society were mandated by a narrow set of role possibilities. Women's roles were defined by the circumstances of their society and by their function in child bearing. The social order of their society was stated by those who controlled the corridors of power.

Revolutions have been the historic recourse of the oppressed and exploited. Such victims have sought to reorder social and political institutions to free themselves from their oppression. The women's movement has teetered on the margins of revolution but has never adopted revolutionary means to complement its revolutionary objectives.

The problem of objectives in the women's movement points up the vacuum of ideology that underlies its origins. Simone de Beauvoir has suggested an ideological position that was certainly not considered by the American movement but that might describe the successes that have evolved. de Beauvoir refers to a "socialism" not like any form of socialism currently in practice. She would make the strategy of the women's movement the rejection of participation as tokens or symbols in existing unequal regimes or political arenas. She further advocates collective action without hierarchies or structures that emulate and reinforce the extant system. The tactics of such a movement, according to de Beauvoir, must be sufficiently broad as to make participation possible for every woman.

Yet an increasingly diverse population of women identifies with the struggle for equality in the workplace and in the family. Today's young women have choices that most women over forty could never have imagined, and older women confront the loss of their familiar identities and the conflicting problems and possibilities of a new kind of freedom. Yet cultural mythology about femaleness restricts their capacity to change. How deep and strong are the taboos on anger, strength, initiative, solitude, and even selfhood for a woman! How glorified still are the virtues of nurturing, selflessness, responsiveness, and adaptability! Do we not find women every day evaluated professionally on their interpretation of these values into work tasks? Yet growth and change require a toughness and a self-respecting selfishness that are "unfeminine."

This identity conflict exists for transitional women as individuals and as a group attempting to define their struggle in terms of the women's movement and as persons living in a time of rapid change and exceptional alienation.

The two decades in which this identity crisis has been brewing reached its apogee with the candidacy of the first woman to enter the arena of presidential politics in the United States. The prominence of Representative Geraldine Ferraro compelled many women to articulate their own dilemma. If the media and the voting public view her candidacy as a legitimate progression of the democratic process, this will be a giant step toward the future of women as full and equal participants in it. Transitional generations of women will give way to the first generation of the New Woman. Further, if the New Woman in power can carry women's culture into the political fabric of a democratic society, the objectives of the women's movement can be the New Society.

Notes

1. *Washington Post,* 30 January 1982.
2. Alvin Toffler, *The Third Wave* (New York: Macmillan, 1980).
3. Ibid.
4. Margaret Mead, *Male and Female* (New York: Morrow, 1949).

APPENDIX A.
Biodemographic Questionnaire

1. Your name _____

2. Date of birth _____

3. Place of birth _____

4. If not born in United States, what is your citizenship? _____

5. Please indicate the state or foreign country in which your parents were born:
   Father _____
   Mother _____

6. If either parent is deceased, please give year of death:
   Father _____ Mother _____

7. Are your parents: 1 2 3 4 5 6 7 8 9
   1. married and living together
   2. married and separated
   3. divorced
   4. widowed

8. Up to age 16, who did you live with mostly?   1 2 3 4 5 6 7 8 9
   1. mother & father
   2. mother & stepfather
   3. stepmother & father
   4. mother only
   5. father only
   6. other

9. How old was your father when you were born?   1 2 3 4 5 6 7 8 9
   1. under 20
   2. 20-25

3. 26-30
4. 31-35
5. 36-40
6. 41 or over

10. How old was your mother when you were born?   1 2 3 4 5 6 7 8 9
    1. under 20
    2. 20-25
    3. 26-30
    4. 31-35
    5. 36-40
    6. 40 or over

11. Do you think of your mother as identified with   1 2 3 4 5 6 7 8 9
    any ethnic minority group?
    1. yes   2. no   write in which _____

12. Do you think of your father as identified with
    any ethnic minority group?
    1. yes   2. no   write in which _____

13. Does your father have an active religious   1 2 3 4 5 6 7 8 9
    affiliation?
    1. yes   2. no

14. Which one?   1 2 3 4 5 6 7 8 9
    1. Catholic   4. Eastern Orthodox   7. Buddist
    2. Protestant   5. Hindu   8. Ethical Culture
    3. Jewish   6. Moslem   9. Other

15. Does your mother have an active religious   1 2 3 4 5 6 7 8 9
    affiliation?
    1. yes   2. no

16. Which one?   1 2 3 4 5 6 7 8 9
    1. Catholic   4. Eastern Orthodox   7. Buddist
    2. Protestant   5. Hindu   8. Ethical Culture
    3. Jewish   6. Moslem   9. Other

17. Do you have an active religious affiliation?   1 2 3 4 5 6 7 8 9
    1. yes   2. no

18. Which one?   1 2 3 4 5 6 7 8 9
    1. Catholic   4. Eastern Orthodox   7. Buddist
    2. Protestant   5. Hindu   8. Ethical Culture
    3. Jewish   6. Moslem   9. Other

19. Indicate the highest level of education   1 2 3 4 5 6 7 8 9
    completed by your father:
    1. grammar school
    2. some high school
    3. high school graduate
    4. technical training without college
    5. some college
    6. college graduate
    7. master's
    8. doctorate (such as Ph.D., Ed.D.)
    9. professional degree (J.D., M.D., D.D.S., L.L.B., etc.)

20. Indicate the highest level of education   1 2 3 4 5 6 7 8 9
    completed by your mother:
    1. grammar school
    2. some high school
    3. high school graduate
    4. technical training without college
    5. some college
    6. college graduate
    7. master's
    8. doctorate (such as Ph.D., Ed.D.)
    9. professional degree (J.D., M.D., D.D.S., L.L.B., etc.)

21. Father's occupation?

22. During your childhood, what was your father's major occupation?

23. Was your mother employed at any time since   1 2 3 4 5 6 7 8 9
    you were born?
    1. yes   2. no

24. If yes, please mark whether your mother was employed during each of
    these periods of your life:

When you were:	full-time	part-time	not employed
5 yrs. or less	1. ____	5. ____	9. _____
6-10 yrs.	2. ____	6. ____	10. _____
11-15 yrs.	3. ____	7. ____	11. _____
16 yrs. or older	4. ____	8. ____	12. _____

25. By and large, how did your mother feel about   1 2 3 4 5 6 7 8 9
    her work?
    1. would have preferred not to work at all
    2. would have preferred a different job
    3. neutral
    4. content with her job
    5. enjoyed her job
    6. not applicable — was not employed

26. What was your father's reaction to your   1 2 3 4 5 6 7 8 9
    mother's working?
    1. would have preferred her not to work at all
    2. would have preferred her to have a different job
    3. neutral
    4. content with her working
    5. very pleased with her work
    6. not applicable — mother not employed or father not in home

27. What is (are) your mother's occupation(s)?

28. Estimate your father's annual income   1 2 3 4 5 6 7 8 9
    when you were a teenager:
    1. below $5,000   5. above $25,000
    2. $5,000-$10,000   6. retired/unemployed
    3. $10,000-$15,000   7. not applicable
    4. $15,000-$25,000

29. Estimate your mother's annual income   1 2 3 4 5 6 7 8 9
    when you were a teenager:
    1. below $5,000   5. above $25,000
    2. $5,000-$10,000   6. retired/unemployed
    3. $10,000-$15,000   7. not applicable
    4. $15,000-$25,000

30. Are you: 1 2 3 4 5 6 7 8 9
    1. an only child   3. middle child
    2. oldest child   4. youngest child

31. Did you date during high school?   1 2 3 4 5 6 7 8 9
    1. yes   2. no

32. If yes to 31, did you "go steady"?   1 2 3 4 5 6 7 8 9
    1. yes   2. no

33. Have you been employed outside your   1 2 3 4 5 6 7 8 9
    home for pay since completing your education?
    1. yes   2. no

34. If yes to 33, please list jobs starting with the most recent:
    1. _____
    2. _____
    3. _____
    4. _____
    5. _____
    6. _____

35. Do you expect to be employed at a later time?   1 2 3 4 5 6 7 8 9
    1. yes   2. no

36. If yes to 35:
    1. When _____
    2. What occupation _____

37. Do you expect to return to school?   1 2 3 4 5 6 7 8 9
    1. yes   2. no

38. If yes to 37, for what course of study or degree?   1 2 3 4 5 6 7 8 9
    1. high school
    2. college, bachelor's degree
    3. master's degree
    4. doctoral degree
    5. professional school program
    6. technical training
    7. not applicable

39. If yes to 37, when do you plan to   1 2 3 4 5 6 7 8 9
return to school?
    1. this year
    2. next year
    3. 2-4 years
    4. 5-7 years
    5. 8-10 years
    6. not applicable

40. When did you decide on your profession?   1 2 3 4 5 6 7 8 9
    1. elementary school
    2. high school
    3. college
    4. after college (while training for another
       career) (specify) _____
    5. after college (while working)

41. When did you first marry?   1 2 3 4 5 6 7 8 9
    1. not married
    2. before college
    3. after college
    4. after college, but not while attending graduate school
    5. during graduate school
    6. after graduate school
    7. other

42. What is your husband's current occupation?

43. What is the highest level of education   1 2 3 4 5 6 7 8 9
completed by your husband?
    1. grammar school
    2. some high school
    3. high school graduate
    4. technical training without college
    5. some college
    6. college graduate
    7. master's
    8. doctorate (such as Ph.D., Ed.D.)
    9. professional degree (J.D., L.L.B., M.D.)

44. If you were to start working now,   1 2 3 4 5 6 7
    the reaction of your husband would be:

    1. very upset
    2. somewhat upset, but he would get over it
    3. mixed feelings—pleased in some ways, displeased in others
    4. indifferent
    5. he would be happy; he wants me to work if I want to
    6. doesn't apply (I'm not married or I'm already working)
    7. he wants me to work, I don't want to work

45. If you were to stop working now, the reaction   1 2 3 4 5 6 7 8
    of your husband would be:

    1. very upset
    2. somewhat upset, but he would get over it
    3. mixed feelings—pleased in some ways, displeased in others
    4. indifferent
    5. he would be happy; he wants me to work if I want to
    6. doesn't apply (I'm not married or I'm already working)
    7. he wants me to work, I don't want to work
    8. doesn't apply (I'm not married or I've already stopped working)

46. For the next five questions, fill in the sentences   1 2 3 4 5 6 7 8 9
    from the list below that applies best:

    1. housewife—mother
    2. employed only before children were born, not after
    3. occasionally employed (every now and then) throughout marriage
       and child rearing
    4. combining marriage and child rearing with steady part-time work
    5. combining marriage and child rearing with a full-time career
    6. marriage and career, without children
    7. not married, career only
    8. not married, having children, but no career
    9. not married, having children and a career

46a. At age 16, which of the situations listed in   1 2 3 4 5 6 7 8 9
    46 would you have preferred?

46b. At age 16, which of the above situations did   1 2 3 4 5 6 7 8 9
    you expect?

46c. Most men would prefer their wives to be   1 2 3 4 5 6 7 8 9
_____ (which of the above)

46d. My mother wanted me to be _____   1 2 3 4 5 6 7 8 9
(which of the above)

46e. Currently I am _____   1 2 3 4 5 6 7 8 9
(which of the above)

47. Please list children by age

	No. of Children	Sex of Children
1. 0-2 years		
2. 3-5 years		
3. 5-7 years		
4. 8-10 years		
5. 11-13 years		
6. 13-17 years		
7. 18-21 years		
8. over 21		

48. Which parent do (did) you respect the most   1 2 3 4 5 6 7 8 9
    1. father   2. mother

49. Which parent would (are) you be most   1 2 3 4 5 6 7 8 9
likely to confide in?
    1. father   2. mother

50. Which parent was the disciplinarian when   1 2 3 4 5 6 7 8 9
you were growing up?
    1. father   2. mother

51. Which parent had the most influence over   1 2 3 4 5 6 7 8 9
how you spent your spare time?
    1. father   2. mother

52. Which parent is more praising of your   1 2 3 4 5 6 7 8 9
accomplishments?
    1. father   2. mother

53. Which parent do you need the most now?   1 2 3 4 5 6 7 8 9
    1. father   2. mother

54. Which parent would you turn to for advice?   1 2 3 4 5 6 7 8 9
    1. father   2. mother

55. Check the five most outstanding characteristics of your father

competent	attractive	intrusive	bright	distant
dominant	submissive	successful	active	ambitious
charming	passive	warm	joiner	leader
tough	shrewd	organizer	traditional	insecure
intimate	status conscious	affectionate	pushy	
involved	repressed	casual	powerful	

56. Check the five most outstanding characteristics of your mother

competent	attractive	intrusive	bright	distant
dominant	submissive	successful	active	ambitious
charming	passive	warm	joiner	leader
tough	shrewd	organizer	traditional	insecure
intimate	status conscious	affectionate	pushy	
involved	repressed	casual	powerful	

57. What qualities about you does your father   1 2 3 4 5 6 7 8 9
    like most? (Choose the *one* he likes *most)*
    1. social characteristics
    2. moral character
    3. intellectual characteristics
    4. physical characteristics

58. What quality about you does your mother   1 2 3 4 5 6 7 8 9
    like most?
    1. social characteristics
    2. moral character
    3. intellectual characteristics
    4. physical characteristics

59. In terms of how well-adjusted I am   1 2 3 4 5 6 7 8 9
    mentally, overall I feel that:
    1. I am frequently skating on thin ice
    2. While there have been difficult times for me, I have done pretty well

3. I have had no more or less difficulty than the average woman
4. I have had much fewer problems than the average woman
5. I have never had any real emotional problems I consider significant

60. Have you ever felt the need for some form of   1 2
    counseling or therapy for problems of an
    emotional nature?
    1. yes   2. no

61. Have you ever gone through therapy counseling?   1 2
    1. yes   2. no

63. Have you ever had any significant problems   1 2
    with anxiety, depression, or other symptoms of
    a psychological nature?
    1. yes   2. no

64. Which of the following most closely describes   1 2 3 4 5
    your involvement in the current women's move-
    ment?
    1. not involved
    2. I've attended some consciousness-raising sessions
    3. I belong to a feminist organization
    4. I participate fully in organization activities
    5. I have been a leader in feminist groups

65. On the scale below, indicate the emotional   1 2 3 4 5 6 7
    difficulty you have experienced resulting from
    your own internal conflicts about being a
    woman:
       none   some   A great deal
    1   2   3   4   5   6   7

66. On the scale below, indicate the amount of   1 2 3 4 5 6 7
    emotional difficulty you have experienced
    resulting from external pressures about your
    being a woman:
       none   some   A great deal
    1   2   3   4   5   6   7

67. Please list what you feel should be 3 main goals of the feminist movement:

APPENDIX B.
Pathological Behaviors as a Function of Sex-Role Attribution[1]

This summarization of three studies of the destructive and even pathological consequences of sex-role expectations and stereotyped identity illustrates many of the issues discussed in Chapters 8, 9, and 10. Although each study was done at a different point during the two decades that frame the contemporary women's movement, they separately and together reflect the social and institutional dysfunctions against which women mobilized themselves for social change.

This paper is a synthesis of three earlier empirical researches conducted independently and at least half a decade apart from one another. Although each study was concerned with a different aspect of sex-role behavior or sex-role expectancy behavior, the studies did not seem to have much coherence among them except in their implications for understanding the effects of sex-role socialization and choice behaviors. Two of the studies, "Drug Abuse and Sex-Role Expectancy Behavior" and "The Personality Dynamics of Adolescent Unwed Mothers," concerned themselves primarily with the way females perceived femaleness and their motivation to achieve. The third, "Sexism in the Student Evaluations," is a study of the effects of dissonance when females and the role in which they are encountered do not "match" the expectancies of others.

The data of these studies do not present isolated or peculiar phenomenon in the larger context of sex-role research findings. Neither as individual studies nor taken together do they present a significantly new contribution to the accumulated plethora of validated, replicated studies on the effects of sex discrimination.

However, when we consider these data together and from the perspective of attribution theory, it may be possible to refine the concept "sex-role socialization" into pragmatic terms amenable to countervention. It is with this objective in prospect, then, that we consider findings that indicate the following:

[1]Presented at the Capitol Area Social Psychological Association Fourth Biennial Meeting, October 28, 1978, in a symposium entitled "Sex Role Behaviors."

152

1. Adolescents selectively determine their drug abuse patterns on the basis of meeting sex-role expectancies.
2. Adolescent females motivated to become pregnant out of wedlock are, to a large degree, attempting to meet sex-role norms that they feel they are not otherwise achieving.
3. Students, male and female, have expectancies of professors and expectancies of females by virtue of which a female professor is cognitively dissonant.

Attribution theory recognizes individuals as agents making choices and in so doing attempting to reconcile those choices with their view of themselves and with the responses of others toward that behavior. Thus, the individual choosing to use drugs (as in the first study) is doing so because it is consistent with a self-perception and the drug-induced behavior elicits social responses that are also consistent with self-perception. On the face of it, this might appear more readily explicable through attribution theory than in studies of drug use (or abuse); the behavior is seldom in conflict with the attitude so that dissonance theory need not be invoked. However, attribution is as significant a factor (as we shall see) as it is in those experiments in which dissonance is the issue resolved through attribution. As Kelley points out: "the questions concern the causes of observed behavior and the answers of interest are those given by the man in the street. The theory also deals with questions of self-perception" (Kellley, Hollander and Hunt, 1976).

Usually, studies of attribution theory involve second- or third-party responses and are based on consistency, expectancy, external pressures, and the reactions of others as determinants of attribution. This conventional interpretation of attribution theory is readily recognizable in the data of student evaluations of female professors (as we shall see), but it is the aspect of "self-perception" noted by Kelley but seldom accessible for laboratory validation that is reflected in the other two studies. It is this aspect of attribution theory that is most closely related to concepts in clinical and developmental psychology at the nexus to which we allude when we speak of "socialization."

Attribution theory implies choice behavior influenced and therefore predicated on social influences. The socialization process (and theories of socialization) incorporates institutional structures, group norms, and social values into the cognitive and affective processes of the young and thus not only produces the social influences but establishes the field of alternatives from which the choice behavior may be selected.

Thus an individual, particularly an adolescent who is struggling with trying out and establishing identity, chooses behaviors and aspires to behaviors attributed by him or her as role-appropriate (unless the individual attributes to himself or herself social deviance).

Choosing Pathological Behaviors

No one chooses to act on something perceived as a "bad for action." Motivation is definitionally predicated on "moving toward," and a person moves toward that which is perceived as a "good for action" (Arnold, 1960). After all, it is the perceptual-cognitive inference from which one attributes any particular value to an event or behavior; and it is this function of attribution as a mediating process in motivation that gives meaningfulness to the situation.

Studies of contraceptive behavior have indicated that one of the greatest obstacles to effective contraceptive behavior is the woman's own perception of herself and her role. According to Sconzoni and McMurray (1972), the view of woman's role as the traditional wife-mother was highly corollary with contraceptive "failure." Kapor-Stanulovic and Lynn (1972) recognized patterns of discrepancy between feminine identification and feminine preference in contraceptive use. They described sex-role identification as "the internalization as aspects of the role appropriate to a given sex and to the unconscious reactions characteristic of that role. Sex role preference refers to the desire to adopt behavior associated with one sex or the opposite." They tested 184 women who had used contraceptives for at least six months and came up with four subsamples: average feminine identification/average feminine preference; high feminine identification/low feminine preference; low feminine identification/high feminine preference; and high feminine identification/high feminine preference. The four groups were compared on contraceptive problems including complaints, side effects, and feelings toward pregnancy. The results indicated that problems associated with contraceptive use increased in two instances: when women are highly feminine or when they have low feminine identification/high feminine preference patterns. High identification/high preference women feel that contraception intrudes into their normally dependent and passive feminine lives. Birth control orients them toward activity and initiative that are foreign to them. According to the Sconzoni and McMurray 1972 data, these would also be the women who are strongly motivated toward pregnancy anyway. For low identification/high preference women, contraceptive use is full of conflicts. Feeling less feminine, they would have little difficulty dealing with contraception except that they value femininity highly and therefore are threatened by their self-image as inadequate females. They rigidly stick to one method of contraception (usually the pill) and release their tension by having frequent complaints and problems. Their strong desire to belong properly with their own sex and their stereotype of feminine fragility includes hypochondria, nervousness, and complaints. On the other hand, women with high feminine identification/low feminine preference see birth control as a carefree experience. They enjoy the active part they take in controlling their bodies. They are seen as a "high risk" group because they experiment with many methods. Kapor-Stanulovic and Lynn (1972) felt that this might reflect an unconscious desire for pregnancy.

McMurray and Sconzoni (1972) cite a similar study done on women testing sex-role stereotypes. In their study, women who possess a "male" or "competency oriented" perception of themselves had fewer children than women with the more traditional female self-concept of "warmth and sensitivity." Also, in view of the fact that every major fertility study shows an inverse relationship between the amount of the wife's work experience and family size, it was significant that among wives with more modern self-concepts, this inverse relationship disappeared. Only among the more traditional women was work duration related to family size. This distinction between work force situation and self-concept vis-à-vis sex-role stereotypes is further bourne out in a study of women who proclaimed themselves feminists and women who by self-definition were not feminists but who worked full time. The former had fewer children and were not as consistently nor as heavily employed as was the sample of traditionalists (Fields and Patrick, 1975).

Newman's 1971 data on unwanted pregnancy and abortion suggest that pregnancies often occur at the points in a women's sexual life cycle when she feels least able to prepare herself contraceptively. Thus, for adolescents, he suggests, pregnancy is often a product of initial or infrequent sexual experience. For divorced women, conception seems to occur shortly after disaffiliation and in the initial stages of a new relationship. These appear to be times when the woman's identity and sense of control of her destiny might be most limited.

Miller's 1973 research on contraceptive use and unwanted pregnancies indicated that on several dimensions associated with feminine sex-role expectancies, such as feminine masochism, submission and dependence, and inability to plan outcomes, there was a relationship with contraceptive failure and lack of pregnancy planning. While Miller did not himself suggest that these "ego factors" were related to feminine role expectance, it is clear from his description of the questions measuring each of the nine factors that they distinguish between active and passive decision making and planning, initiative versus reaction, and other typical dichotomies.

All these studies indicate that sex-role anxiety or a self-perception of sex-role inadequacy along with the inference of pregnancy as a confirmation of femaleness may well contribute to a motivation for pregnancy. If carried one step further via attribution theory, then, the uncertain, anxious adolescent female attributes to pregnancy the social power of validating her as a sex-appropriate adult.

Adolescent Unwed Mothers

A study of the personality dynamics of adolescent unwed mothers utilizing a measurement of achievement motivation that analyzes motive orientation into active/passive, positive/negative modes of operation suggests that for adolescent unwed mothers pregnancy has been an action undertaken for resolution of conflict over sex role identity (Fields, 1964).

The institutionalized unwed mothers were compared with sexually active but never-pregnant adolescents of the same age and other demographic characteristics who were institutionalized for reasons other than pregnancy. Story Sequence Analysis was done on Thematic Apperception Test protocols consisting of ten TAT cards for fifty young women aged 15 through 19, Caucasian, U.S. born, eighth grade through postsecondary education levels, residing in the Midwest for all or most of their lives.

While the control subjects (who were institutionalized for deviant behaviors ranging from running away from home to armed robbery) exhibited the significantly high proportions of scores typical of patients with personality disorders, neither group scored in the positive range of achievement motivation. The controls deviated more extensively from the standardization norms than did the unwed mothers, as might be expected given the nature of their preinstitutional behaviors. There were some interesting differences between the two groups, however, suggesting that the unwed mothers, unlike their delinquent counterparts, were strongly valuing traditional feminine role behavior.

The negativism of the unwed mother is of a more consistently passive variety. The quality of their negativism differs despite a quantitative similarity to the controls. The unwed mothers exhibit below-average motivation for achievement, for interpersonal relationships, for dealing with adversity, and in discerning between right and wrong.

Adolescents who become unwed mothers exhibit greater dependency, passivity, lack of goal orientation, desire to manipulate others, and an ability to deal with any kind of adversity. They would appear to be women with different attitudes and behavior from their peers who are not pregnant and not institutionalized and from their peers who are classified as "delinquent." This finding suggests that their pregnancy is not the result of some temporary need but is a behavior consistent with their overall motivational dynamics.

Content analysis of the imports also suggests that unwed mothers are particularly prone to perceiving relationships with others as a means of self-gratification and are likely to manipulate others into providing this. They consider passivity to be the major requisite of feminine role behavior and are apt to consider others as sources of worry, bewilderment, and annoyance. They have little or no heterosexual initiative and view behaviors in dichotomous terms rather than androgynous ones. Rather than act on and react to situations and relationships, their mode of operation is one of waiting, accepting, and avoiding confrontation.

This pattern of negative passivity was much more specific for the unwed mothers than it was for the controls. Although this may be a consequence of the variety of offenses for which the controls were incarcerated, it is also possible that the young women in the control group who scored highest in negative passivity may at some later date also become unwed mothers. The pattern of negative passivity was much stronger and more consistent among this sample (adolescent unwed mothers) than is any particular pattern among the control group and is certainly not evidenced among the standardization samples (see Table 1).

In many respects, these adolescent unwed mothers, with no knowledge of the Broverman studies of clinicians' attribution of health or illness via sex-role dichotomized behaviors (Broverman, Vogel, et al., 1972), attributed successful femininity and thus successful personhood for female people to the same characteristics as clinicians held for "healthy women." Their responses to various situations were characterized by a stereotyped "feminine dependency" and will-lessness. Typical imports derived from the stories of adolescent unwed mothers carry the message that "lesser goals are preferable because they do not affect personal worth," "failure just happens," "success occurs through magic or other supernatural happenings," "wrong intentions are not carried out because one lacks courage," and "good relations are the result of fortuitous happenings — or are broken for no reason." As Broverman et al. study (1972) pointed out:

Table 1

	Unwed Mothers			Controls		
	Active	Passive	Totals	Active	Passive	Totals
Category I: Achievement, goals						
Positive	12	27	14	13	1	14
Negative	14	40	54	13	32	49
Totals	26	42	68	30	33	63
Category II: Right and wrong						
Positive	67	27	8	7	2	9
Negative	4	8	12	5	10	15
Totals	10	10	10	12	12	24
Category III: Human relationships						
Positive	6	8	14	9	23	32
Negative	23	85	108	26	48	74
Totals	29	93	122	35	71	106
Category IV: Reaction to adversity						
Positive	1	2	3	3	1	4
Negative	9	34	43	24	27	51
Totals	9	34	43	24	27	51
Totals	74	179	253	101	143	244

. . . healthy women differ from healthy men [as clinicians view them — ed. note] by being more sul missive, less independent, less adventurous, less objective, more easily influenced, less aggressive, less competitive, more excitable in minor crises, more emotional, more conceited about their appearance, and having their feelings easily hurt (p. 72).

The continued high incidence of adolescent pregnancy out of wedlock even into this decade of access to family planning information and abortion seems to be testimony to the pervasive and pathological potential of sex-role stereotypes. While the incidence of adolescent unwed births has declined among black teenagers, it has increased among white adolescents. The persistence of this self-concept seems to have even defied the changes brought on by a resurgent feminist movement. The fact of increase in adolescent births outside of wedlock is coincidental with a decade in which women have, ironically in this case, defied sex-role norms to demand freedom from the centuries-old constraints that limited their adolescent options to child bearing, inside or outside of wedlock, but no other behavior consistent with a positive sex-role identity.

Persistence of this stereotype and self-concepts demanding adherence to its outmoded dimensions seems perverse and pathological but demonstrates the holding power and long-term effect of sex-role attribution.

Six years after the study of the unwed mothers, at a time when adolescent behavior had come to be characterized by dissidence and deviance and seemed to have challenged and violated every presumption about role behavior, be it age or sex, a study was conducted in southern California on drug abuse among adolescents.

Out of a sample population of 204 high school students from a middle-class community in southern California, 27% admitted to drug use. Of these, males made up slightly more than half the total. The study revealed that there was a significant difference in choice of drugs corollary with sex of user. Young women chose barbiturates and hallucinogens more frequently than did their male counterparts, who used amphetamines almost exclusively. Through interviews with these adolescent drug abusers it was learned that the behavioral objective for drug use differed by sex of respondent. The selections and the expected effects, however, were consistent with sex-role stereotyping. A search of the literature further disclosed that sex-role differences in selective choice of drug abuse is not of recent origins but that earlier researchers found that sex-role identity conflicts related to drug abuse.

This study indicated that drug use by adolescents might be a function of their anxieties over self-image inconsistencies with sex-role expectancies.

Drugs and Sex-Role Stereotypes

In the report of the President's Commission on Law Enforcement, Task Force on Narcotics and Drug Abuse, there is a reference to a work by Kolb (1962) that reports that "women outnumbered men as addicts in the 19th century." This information raises some questions that are unanswered in the other literature. First, whether the rate by sex has been studied in an ongoing fashion, and if so, whether the proportion is the same; second, what was there about nineteenth-century life in the United States that militated toward heavy use of opiates by women? Then, of course, the further issue, which seems implicit in the choice of this "fact," how is it that deviance of women is so readily accountable statistically? Further, in the same article it is noted that "persons in certain occupations with traditions of opiate use (entertainment, prostitution, etc.) will be expected more often to develop use and also dependency" (Task Force Report, p. 49).

In the same report, there are summary descriptions of the research findings on social milieau corollaries with drug abuse (opiate type) and personality studies of opiate users. The findings, although often contradictory, include some consensual conclusions. As regards ethnicity and poverty as correlates of drug addiction, the report states that "an ethnic group is not predisposed to opiate use by virtue of any inherent racial or ethnic criminal culture or weakness. Rather, it can express an attempt at personal adjustment — or a personal reaction to maladjustment — which also has certain meanings or symbolic value for the using group. The opiate dependent behavior of the underprivileged is a response of the persons to forces generated outside their ethnic group . . ." (ibid., p. 30).

As regards the personality of the opiate habitue, the report states that "there are many descriptions of the personality of addicts, most of them arguing that addicts lack initiative and self-reliance and are passive, inadequate and immature . . . the best demonstrated trait is that of a kind of sociability which makes group membership important . . . the addiction itself was functional in the sense that it served a purpose for them, representing an 'adjustment,' a relief of pain, and perhaps a less arduous . . . road of life during periods of adolescent developmental stress . . . general unhappiness, difficulty in sexual identification and poor interpersonal techniques are also confirmed" (ibid., p. 51).

Opiate addicts who were imprisoned were studied by Phillips and Delhees (1968) and Paprocki (1960) using Cattell's IPAT 16 PF personality questionnaire. Although the group was all male, the profile for both groups denotes the following personality factor loadings: emotionally less stable, submissive, serious, sensitive, suspicious, apprehensive, high anxiety, emotionally responsive, and high neuroticism. The fact that the users were imprisoned and in various kinds of treatment and rehabilitation programs may have some contaminating effects on the accentuation of these particular factors. However, these findings fit closely to those described in the Task Force Report as characteristics of opiate users.

These descriptions of the personal and social conditions of opiate addicts bear a striking resemblance to the characteristics attributed by clinicians for appraisal of mental health in women. From the study by Broverman et al., it is apparent that concepts of social desirability for a mature healthy woman differ significantly from concepts of health held as standards for "adults" and that the latter coincide closely with the standards for men:

> For instance . . . clinicians are more likely to suggest that healthy women differ from healthy men by being more submissive, less independent, less adventurous, more easily influenced, less aggressive, less competitite, more excitable in minor crises, having their feelings more easily hurt, being more emotional, more conceited about their appearance, less objective and disliking math and science (Broverman, Vogel et al., 1972).

Taken together, these findings would suggest that females, especially adolescent girls who aspire to social desirability and are thus experiencing problems of sexual identification with the stereotypical female role, might choose to use those drugs that would appear to produce the desired behavioral effects. That is, such persons will use barbiturates and hallucinogens more frequently. For similar reasons, they may have, in the past, been most likely to use opiates. Since the availability of barbiturates and tranquilizers, which produce behavioral effects similar to opiates and permit oral dosage rather than the consequent disfigurement of repeated injection, it might be assumed that women drug users would be apt to prefer them.

The effects of barbiturates, opiates, tranquilizers, and hallucinogens would correspond to expected role behaviors for females (i.e., passivity resulting from apathy; relief of anxiety, tension; diminishment of the sex, hunger, and other primary drives).

Becker (1970) describes the choice of drug use as a product of "wanting to experience these subjective effects; they take them, to put it colloquially, because they want to get 'high.'"

> Even if physiologically observable effects are substantially the same in all members of the species, individuals can vary widely in those to which they choose to pay attention . . . a great variety of effects may be singled out by the user as desirable or pleasurable, as the effects for which he has taken the drug . . . how a person experiences the effects of a drug depends greatly on the way others define those effects for him (ibid.).

These descriptions of drug use, preference, personality dimensions, and convergence with female sex-role stereotype would suggest that not only the nineteenth-century women described by Kolb are heavy narcotics users, but that there might be a continuing relationship (perhaps even socio-historically a direct corollary) between unrealistic sex-role expectancies for women and their involvement in drugs.

There are both subjective reasons for taking particular drugs and for purposes of expected behavioral outcome and there are initiating circumstances for choosing to use drugs at all; these might relate to anxiety in sexual identification, particularly in adolescence. If these kinds of psychosocial interactions relating to sex-role differences affect drug use, then one might expect a different pattern to be extant for male users, although we have found no studies describing patterns of drug abuse by sex (apart from the statistics on male/female addiction described by Kolb).

Reviewing the literature on the use of amphetamines, the Task Force Report (1969) describes them as

> widely prescribed by physicians in attempts to reduce weight, control fatigue, overcome minor depressions. . . . In addition to supervised medical use, amphetamines are apparently widely employed in self-medication by persons seeking to combat lethargy, overweight, and fatigue . . . (p. 2a).

Further:

> In another study, amphetamines were given to delinquents as part of a treatment effort and under these drugs the boys were found to show better adjustment and better work compared to delinquents not so treated (ibid., p. 30).

The uses and effects of methamphetamines are described by Sher (1966), under the classification "Amphetamines." Since methamphetamine is not the only kind or form of "upper," it would hardly be accurate to describe its uses and effects as characterizing the whole range of them. Some "uppers," such as dexedrine, are used and prescribed as antidepressants; they are believed to be physiologically habituating, and methamphetamine users do develop tolerance levels. It is noteworthy that the effects of "meth" described by Sher (1966) are effects of and on masculine sexual behavior: "One very important aspect of the use and appeal of amphetamines is its employment initially as a sexual concomitant or stimulant. . . ."

Further on in the article, Sher describes Theatrogenic Abusers and includes synthetic uppers and downers as habituating and resulting in a "continuous vague state of confusion, giddiness, psychomoter awkwardness and sensory irritability" (ibid.).

Patricia Sexton, in her book *The Feminized Male,* describes the contradictions extant for adolescent boys between the requisites of school and the social definitions of masculinity. Boys are told, on the one hand, that the marketplace they will eventually enter expects them to be ruggedly competitive; in school, on the other hand, they are told that in order to earn the "gold star" or the teacher's approval, they must passively study and be "good." The elaboration and extension of irrelevant historical sex roles for men are reiterated in the Broverman study, which indicates that clinically valued traits for men include independence, aggression, ambition, lack of emotionality, dominance, competitiveness, activity, self-confidence, and adventurousness.

Given the subjective nature of drug choice and effects, it would seem reasonable to expect that "uppers" might well appear to be an appropriate adient for a boy concerned with fulfilling the requisites of socially desirable behavior for a male.

Sex Difference and Drug Use

In surveying the population of ninth through twelfth graders in one high school, from a sample of 204 students aged 14 through 18, 27% admitted to having used one or more of four kinds of illegal narcotics during the preceding year. Of this group, boys made up 15.6% and girls amounted to 11.3% of the total. Of the total user population, 97.9% had used marijuana anywhere from 1 to 50 or more times; 48.1% reported using "whites" (amphetamines, also called "uppers"); 39.2% reported having used "reds" (seconals, a barbiturate also called "downers") during the past year; and 26.9% had used LSD.

Of this group there were some persistent differences by sex in use patterns as well as in questionnaire responses.

Although 11 of the girls reported having used "reds," and 6 of them had used them between 10 and 50 plus times, only 3 boys reported having used reds, and none of them had used them more than 9 times. The difference almost reversed itself in the use of "whites." Twenty-two boys had used amphetamines, and of these, 13 had used them upward of 10 times. Among the girls, only 7 had used "whites" that often, and the other 7 who had used them at all had done so less than 10 times. Eleven girls reported having used LSD, while only 2 boys had done so.

There was also a significant difference in age patterns for drug use by sex. While the largest number of boys using drugs were among the 16 year olds, and the least number among those who were 17 and older, the heaviest users among the girls were in the 17 and older age groups.

Sixteen of the girls had used marijuana; only 7 of the boys had done so. This was also statistically significant.

Taken together, the proportions of girls were significant for using drugs that purported to produce euphoria, lessen aggressiveness objectivity, and increase emotional responsiveness and submissiveness. The girls also showed considerably greater versatility in drug use. Although they comprised a smaller percentage of the sample of users, they represented the significant majority of those who had used drugs 50 or more times within the previous year. Fourteen girls fell into this category, while only 6 boys admitted to such heavy use.

Heavy use among the boys was almost exclusively with "whites." Thirteen boys (as large a proportion of the male sample as hallucinogen users among females) reported having used "whites" more than 10 times.

Referring again to the subjective nature of drug choices and effects among users, one could speculate that boys using drugs are choosing to use drugs that act as a sex stimulant, combat lethargy, overcome fatigue, and control weight. Since "concern with appearance" is supposedly a female trait, weight control by the usual means would appear inconsistent with the masculine image. Lethargy with its attendant passivity would also be inconsistent with the masculine image. Fulfilling work standards, as set for males, might also be made more possible by increased action potential.

Sex Difference Evidenced in Attitudes

In responding to the questionnaire, there were some striking sex differences in some of the answers. These differences obtained for the total group, which included users and nonusers. The positions represented by these responses may have some relationship to the choices of using drugs at all and to the apparent sex differences in choosing which drugs to use.

In response to the question "Most people who use stimulants like 'pep pills' and 'speed' can stop any time they want to," twice as many males as females checked the category "cannot decide." A significant majority of the total group rejected the statement. Of these, 20% more girls rejected the statement than did boys.

Question 13 required checking levels of agreement ranging from "strongly agree" to "strongly disagree" with this statement: "There is little use writing to public officials or trying to get help from public agencies because they really aren't interested in the problems of the average person." This question has sometimes been used to measure feelings of personal political efficacy versus alienation. Twice as many females as males responded by checking "disagree" on this statement. Interestingly, those who identified as having used marijuana significantly more often selected this response to the statement than did users of other drugs. This would suggest that marijuana users feel that there is more possibility for redress of grievance by "working through the system" than do users of other drugs. It would also suggest that girls as a group are more likely to feel this way.

More boys than girls felt that they had been pressured to "turn on"; in fact, 20% more boys reported having experienced this kind of pressure.

Among the users there was significant rejection for the statement "There are times when it is all right to take amphetamines and barbiturates even if a physician hasn't prescribed them for you." However, the rejection came essentially from those using LSD and/or marijuana, with only 2 of the amphetamine users and none of the barbiturate users rejecting the statement. For the total group, significantly more boys had accepted the statement than had girls.

Adolescents attribute power to drugs. In the typical condition of powerlessness that characterizes childhood and striving for adult identity, adolescents seek the "magic" of "drug power." This sample, obtained in 1969-70, reflects the then extant societal norms for "feminine" and "masculine" behaviors. It would be interesting now to learn if the new standards of aggressivity and initiative for women are reflected in adolescents' subjective choices of drugs to abuse.

Second-Party Attribution: Bias against Nontraditional Women

We have considered evidence of self-destructive behaviors emanating from attributing resolution of sex-role identity conflicts to changes in one's own physical condition and to chemically induced behavioral change. Now we consider the more conventional examples of attribution theory in sex-role bias.

Sexism in Student Evaluations of Professors

Women college teachers suffer from sex discrimination in student evaluations. According to a study conducted at Clark University, students disagree by sex on what constitutes a good professor; but there is no differential between male and female students in evaluating female professors as significantly less able than their male counterparts to encourage students to study, to communicate in class, and to be available outside class. Male professors, according to the students, made them feel more comfortable in class.

Although women professors were evaluated as highly as their male colleagues in "mastery of subject" and in specific areas of teaching, they were significantly lower than men in evaluation of overall teaching performance. This is clearly an instance of the whole being less than the sum of the parts. In analyzing these results, we might consider that sex-role stereotyping through students' socialization experiences produces the gestalt product.

If students are responding to the teaching environment in distinguishable sex-role stereotyped patterns (differential expectations from professors consistent with sex-role socialization), it is almost corollary to expect that their reaction to professors will reflect their differential expectations from males and females as such. This study suggests that in institutions that have a small proportion of women faculty and where women faculty, because of their junior rank, are primarily teaching lower-division courses, there is a greater likelihood of their receiving poor student evaluations.

That men and women are evaluated differently has been established through a plethora of studies ranging from McKee and Sherriff's 1957 study to contemporary evaluations of women by supervisors in every sphere of the working world. It is evident that sex-role stereotyping affects judgments of role-appropriate behaviors and that this in turn affects evaluations of individual job performance. In the university setting, discrimination against women authors was studied and substantiated through replication studies in various universities (Goldberg, 1968), and Jessie Bernard (1954) suggested in *Academic Women* that women professors in the social sciences are more likely to have their credibility challenged through student resistance than would women in other fields because of the controversial nature of the issues they cover in which women's opinions carry little weight.

Sex typing is part of the child's cognitive development, according to studies by Kohlberg (Kohlberg and Ziegler, 1956). This typing proceeds through stages during which even inanimate objects acquire masculinity or femininity according to their usage and associations, until social roles and personal selves have finally integrated the values and attributes associated with sex type. This thesis could easily account for the freshman college students' expectations of masculine professors and their confusion in assimilating the apparent contradictions between "woman" and "professor." This would readily be reinforced for those college students who, in the course of the ensuing years, increasingly meet male professors predominantly at the higher levels of scholarship and prestige. According to Graham (1959):

> Women constitute about 18% of the staffs of institutions of higher education, being distributed principally at small colleges and universities . . . mak(ing) up only 1% of the professors in elite graduate departments (p. 356).

Expectations of female role fulfillment are expectations of a nurturant "mother figure" who uncritically accepts diverse behaviors, is supportive and accommodating (Wikler, 1975). The professional role calls for analytical and critical behaviors, and with increasing severity with the increase of grade level from freshman to graduate student (Strong, 1971). Since, as Jessie Bernard points out, success in role performance depends on the responses of those in complementary roles, the female professor is further inhibited in her assumption of professorial behaviors by the reactions of her students when they do not accept her professional role. Added to this are the problems of collegial discrimination and her uniqueness in a minority group within the institution and in the larger society. These complications, taken together, become one aspect of the vicious circle.

Bernard describes an experiment carried out at the University of Pennsylvania in which two young people, a male and a female, made presentations together to a class of undergraduates. The findings indicated that the young woman had less impact on the class than had the young man, and that she evoked much less reaction from the students. One of the conclusions of the study was that whether or not the students did learn more from the male, he certainly got them more emotionally involved in his presentation, and they tended to accept what he said as "fact" to a greater degree than they did the statements of the female.

The initial emphasis on equalizing academic job opportunities for women signaled the entrance and (in some cases) re-entrance of academic women into the institutions of higher education as untenured assistant professors. As graduate schools began to accept and confer degrees on more women students in the early 1970s, women as a group became the last hired. Marlowe (in Denmark, 1974) points out:

> Under affirmative action, more women had to be invited for job interviews, and more women were hired. Then the university

formulated a policy requiring that no more than the majority of faculty in a department be tenured without exceptional cause. Thus, the recently hired women taken on to redress past discrimination, will be the first to experience what the university indelicately refers to as "nonreappointment" . . . departments are supposed to have certain percentages of full, associate, and assistant professors . . . most new people taken on will be at the more economical assistant professor level. . . . Mainly men are in the senior group and the new women assistant professors are stuck in a revolving door (Denmark, 1974).

There are two major passageways past the revolving door: (1) through publications, and (2) through teaching evaluations by peers and students. In recent years the institution of blind review procedures in most academic journals has increased the number of publications by women. However, the fact remains that most women are employed in institutions that are lower division and undergraduate in character, where the emphasis is on teaching rather than scholarship, and few women ever get the opportunity to involve themselves in the kind of scholarly research that brings academic rewards and glory. The second passageway—student and peer evaluations of teaching—contains another stumbling block for women. The present study indicates that student discrimination in evaluating female professors is empirically measurable and that this behavior provides an insurmountable blockage in the second passageway past the revolving door toward tenure and senior status.

Background of the Study

This research was carried out at Clark University during the academic year 1974-75. At that time the university had 243 faculty members, of whom 13 women were full-time at assistant professor rank or above. In the academic year 1972 -73 there had been 16 women at these ranks, and although the proportion of full professors had increased slightly, the total number had declined. There had been no established system of student evaluation of faculty. Each department was charged with establishing its own system of incorporating student evaluations. Some departments had devised empirical questionnaires; others, like Sociology, had an erratic system of sending letters to students soliciting opinions on professors slated for consideration for renewal or tenure. Since all respondents were provided anonymity, there was no way of ascertaining whether the same persons solicited were indeed the respondents. At the other extreme, the Physics and Chemistry departments had developed a rather elaborate system of questionnaires, computerized responses categorized on several continua, interviews, and peer assessments.

The full-time student body of Clark University at the time of this data collection numbered 2,000. A course evaluation-professor evaluation survey questionnaire was distributed to 720 students, almost equally divided between male and female, and including 228 freshman, 153 sophomore, 149 junior, 159 senior, 17 graduate, and 2 special students.

Thirty professors agreed to cooperate. Of these 30, 6 were women. This resulted in a significantly higher proportion of the women faculty participating in the study—a necessary condition if the results were to be at all generalizeable.

Findings

The questionnaire consisted of 32 evaluation questions and demographic data on major, sex of student, sex of professor, grade level, size of class, structure of class (e.g., seminar vs. lecture), experience of courses in this department, and geographic origins. Several demographic factors correlated significantly for several of the questions, and intercorrelations between questions varied significantly for particular factors. For instance, the higher the students' level (i.e., graduate students more than freshmen), the higher the correlation between the estimation of the instructor and the amount to which the instructor encouraged new perspectives. Graduate students also tended to rate their professors significantly higher in communication skills than did undergraduates.

Differences by sex of student were significant in several instances, as were correlations with geographic origins. The latter may be a function of smaller cells in the chi square formula, or regression phenomenon. Similarly, the differences by grade level, particularly considering the much smaller size of the graduate student group, were concentrated in 3 classes out of the 40 classes surveyed and therefore had a greater chance of homogeneity.

Sex differences between professors loomed as the major producer of significant differences in student response. Only a couple of responses differed statistically significantly by sex of student, and these seemed also to relate to the pattern of differentiation between male and female professors. Table 2 summarizes the data for each question in terms of responses to sex of professor. Despite the fact that students evaluated their male and female professors as equal in mastery of subject, availability, communicative

Table 2

Question	(scale)	Mm[a]	Mf[b]	chi²	Sig. level
1. Mastery of subject	(1-9)	7.96	8.19	2.77	.10
2. Enthusiasm	(1-9)	7.42	7.50	.59	.50
3. Availability to students	(1-9)	6.82	6.39	1.59	.25
4. Ability to communicate	(1-9)	7.82	6.878	1.16	.25
5. Preparedness for class	(1-9)	7.82	7.66		
6. Interest in students	(1-9)	7.05	7.04		
7. Effective use of a/v aids	(1-9)	6.00	7.19	3.846	.05
8. Assigns suitable work	(1-9)	6.92	6.94		
9. Effective course projects	(1-9)	6.21	6.93	10.91	.001
10. Class meetings worthwhile	(1-9)	7.13	6.73	2.65	.25
11. Accessible and interested	(1-5)	3.0	2.79		
12. Fair criticism	(1-5)	2.67	2.02		
13. Encourages further study (yes = 1; no = 2)		Females rated favorably at a ratio of 2 to 1. Males rated favorably at a ratio of 3 to 1.			
14. Regular attendance	(1-4)	1.58	1.91	1.648	.05
15. Good presentation (low favorable)	(1-5)	1.76	1.96		.25
16. Communication (low favorable)	(1-5)	1.80	2.00	.741	.50
17. Encourages new perspectives (low favorable)	(1-5)	1.71	1.97	1.73	.25
18. Encourages questions (low favorable)	(1-5)	1.83	1.93		
19. Concerned about understanding (low favorable)	(1-5)	1.82	2.01	1.371	.25
20. Amount learned (low favorable)	(1-5)	2.18	2.32	.484	.50
21. Responsive to conflicting ideas (low favorable)	(1-5)	2.11	2.22		
22. Comfort in class (low favorable)	(1-5)	1.62	1.40		
23. Estimate of instructor	(1-9)	7.37	6.93		.05 (T-test = .02)
24. General estimate of course	(1-9)	6.50	6.08		.02 T-test

[a]Mean for male professors.
[b]Mean for female professors.
On questions 1, 6, 11, 12, 18, 21, 22, the chi square distribution did not warrant working out a significance figure.

effectiveness, interest in students, and many other qualities, they nonetheless statistically significantly estimated their male instructors as better than their female instructors, and evaluated significantly more highly male-taught courses.

Students seemed to feel that women professors used audiovisual aids more effectively, gave more effective course projects to carry out, and were more enthusiastic.

As for differences in responses relating to sex of students, the only statistically significant response was that concerning questions and discussions. Female students significantly more often felt that questions and discussions were being encouraged; their male counterparts did not (significant at the .02 level).

By correlating responses to grouped questions we find some interesting differences between male and female students' subjective appraisals of professors. The more comfortable a male felt in his class, the more interested he felt the instructor to be in the students in that class, and the better the course was, the more he learned from that course. The male student also estimated the course as better if questions and discussion were encouraged, while the responses of female students demonstrated no correlation between these criteria. Since female students were more likely to feel that questions and discussions were being discouraged, they tended to be less discriminating in relating such circumstances to other criteria of course evaluation or professorial value.

Differences between groups of student by year in school were apparent in comparison of means and standard deviations (see Table 3). Graduate students tended to rate their professors more highly than did undergraduates. The fact that the professors of these graduate students were males may have contributed to the overall difference in ratings of male and female professors. Graduate students were also situated in small seminar classes, which did get overall higher ratings from all students than did the larger lecture courses.

While most of the estimates of professors placed them at the slightly-above-average level (7.00 +), graduate students rated their professors as "superior." Course estimates ran lower than estimates of professors generally (see Table 4).

The interquestion correlations provided interesting differences among students with different majors. These data will not be considered in depth here, but they are mentioned because these differentiations imply that different combinations of qualities contribute to a professor's higher or lower estimate by students enrolled in social sciences contrasted with students

Table 3

Question	Freshmen mean	Freshmen s.d.	Sophomores mean	Sophomores s.d.	Juniors mean	Juniors s.d.	Seniors mean	Seniors s.d.	Graduates mean	Graduates s.d.	Special mean	Special s.d.
1	8.05		7.98	1.35	7.66	1.52	7.54	1.87	8.52	.717	9.00	0.00
2	7.46		7.74	1.70	7.17	1.87	7.34	1.89	8.47	.80	9.00	0.00
3	5.43		6.52	2.47	6.00	2.67	6.22	2.35	7.05	2.43	.50	2.12
4	7.07		6.94	2.05	6.678	2.06	6.84	2.07	7.70	1.40	8.50	0.707
5	7.78		7.92	1.40	7.470	1.84	7.39	1.86	8.17	1.42	9.00	0.
6	6.93		6.84	2.05	6.94	2.14	6.99	2.06	8.23	1.03	6.50	2.12
7	5.96		6.19	2.55	6.15	2.44	5.95	2.51	4.76	3.41	6.50	2.12
8	6.69		6.91	2.09	6.91	1.91	6.83	1.94	7.52	2.71	7.00	2.82
9	5.46		6.25	2.42	6.37	2.30	6.50	2.37	7.35	2.52	7.00	1.41
10	7.01		6.98	2.13	6.85	1.94	6.71	2.17	8.11	1.11	9.00	0.
11	3.36		2.68	1.83	2.22	1.73	2.57	1.81	1.64	1.16	2.00	1.414
12	2.82		1.81	1.57	1.85	1.63	1.81	1.61	1.58	1.32	5.00	0.
13	1.15		1.30	0.631	1.28	0.60	1.21	0.688	1.29	0.470	1.00	0.
14	3.39		2.77	0.949	2.56	1.07	2.44	1.15	2.11	1.21	3.50	0.707
15	1.66		1.41	0.557	1.60	0.74	1.45	0.55	1.35	0.493	2.00	0.
16	1.67		1.71	0.964	1.83	0.947	1.88	1.01	1.52	0.874	1.00	0.
17	1.71		1.81	1.05	1.95	1.055	1.91	0.93	1.82	0.809	1.00	0.
18	1.91		1.95	1.04	1.81	0.93	1.92	0.99	1.29	0.470	1.50	0.707
19	1.85		1.90	0.958	1.79	0.908	1.83	0.89	1.47	0.624	2.00	1.41
20	1.79		1.85	0.76	1.81	0.996	1.97	1.00	1.94	0.659	1.50	0.707
21	2.09		1.81	1.21	2.04	1.332	2.03	1.07	2.00	0.061	1.50	0.707
22	1.94		1.88	1.04	1.89	0.938	2.02	1.06	1.94	1.78	1.50	0.707
23	2.52		2.24	1.30	2.19	1.243	2.26	1.28	1.94	1.88	1.50	0.707
24	6.95		6.75	2.37	6.68	2.19	6.87	2.05	7.58	1.87	7.00	2.82
25	6.12		6.29	2.45	6.26	2.09	6.31	2.13	7.23	2.25	7.00	2.82
26	1.43		1.72	0.982	2.17	1.15	2.19	0.903	3.00	0.935	2.00	1.41
27	1.85		1.79	1.15	1.86	1.072	1.91	1.22	1.41	0.618	1.50	0.707
28	1.14		1.26	0.559	1.188	0.553	1.11	0.584	1.23	0.437	1.00	0.

Table 4

Question	Mean of Soph., Jr., Sr.	Mean of Freshman
1	7.72	8.05
2	7.32	7.46
4	6.82	7.07
5	7.59	7.78
6	6.92	6.93
9	6.37	5.46
10	6.84	7.01
14	2.49	3.36
15	1.82	2.82
20	1.80	1.67
21	1.89	1.71

majoring in humanities or the physical sciences/math groupings. This tends to support the statements by Jessie Bernard, quoted earlier in this paper, regarding the particular differences between social sciences and humanities or physical sciences in the role of women professors. One of the statistically significantly higher ratings accorded male professors was on the item "encourages students to further study this subject" (.05 significance level). Graduate students estimate the overall worth of a professor corollary with the professor's capacity to encourage students to study the subject further.

A study conducted in 1973 by Huber and Ferber at a large midwestern university with 1,291 respondents showed that the majority of the students who expressed sex preference for instructors preferred men professors and that female students expressed this preference even more strongly than did male students. In ranking former professors, men ranked their women professors as having been less adequate than were their male professors (see Table 5).

The Goldberg 1968 studies of college students' responses to articles authored by women has been replicated many times since then, and the findings, while sometimes differing from Goldberg's, have most often and most recently been supportive. That experiment illustrated the distorting effect of the stereotypic belief in women's intellectual inferiority, discrimination by female students against female scholars, and the general sensitivity of students to the author's sex as indicative of content credibility.

Table 5

**Men and Women Students' Preference
for Men or Women Teachers by Type of Section**

	Large Lecture		Lecture/Discussion		Quiz	
	Men	Women	Men	Women	Men	Women
	%		%		%	
Prefer men teachers 1, 2	40	38	21	31	15	26
3	58	60	71	65	72	70
Prefer women teachers 4	2	3	9	3	13	5

Note: 1 = strongly prefer man teacher; 3 = no preference; 4 = strongly prefer woman teacher. I have recalculated this table from Farber and Huber, 1975, table 2, p. 956.

Some aspects of our findings demonstrate the complexities inherent in deriving an estimate of teaching ability from student evaluations. Obviously, students evaluate professors as much out of the nexus of their experience, socialization, and family patterns as they do on the objective behaviors of the teacher in the classroom. It is difficult, if not impossible, to segregate one aspect.

Some studies indicate that student evaluation of professors is highly correlated to classroom style. Our data substantiate this, in that those students who were enrolled in smaller seminar classes evaluated their professors higher than those involved in large lectures. In one case, in fact, graduate students evaluated a woman professor significantly higher than did her undergraduate class—one of the striking differences being class structure and thus classroom style. Since this was the only female professor in our sample who taught a graduate course, it is impossible to generalize from this example, but it is suggestive in that she was highly valued for enthusiasm, warmth, and communication in the small seminar, and not considered remarkable in those qualities by the undergraduates. It is possible that the classroom style permissible in seminar structures is more consistent than large lecture style with female sex-role stereotypes and thus with student expectancies of female professorial behaviors. Wikler (1975) suggests this in her study:

Since women, *qua* women, are expected to be nurturant, expressive and warm, the lack of expression of these qualities by female faculty may be perceived by students as withholding her "natural" female characteristics of warmth and expressiveness. Contrarily, if she possesses the male characteristics such as forcefulness, competence, and decisiveness, she runs the risk of being perceived as aggressive, insensitive and cold. But what if the female professor is warm and responsive? To the extent that she is perceived as fitting the sex role stereotype, she is likely to be intellectually devalued compared to men and open to possible manipulation by students (pp. 7-8).

Wikler also notes that her subjects who were faculty women at the University of California, Santa Cruz, considered expressions of sexism to be exacerbated by larger class sizes. Wikler's interviewees stated that

large lectures require "male" traits such as a strong and commending voice, decisiveness and an authoritative posture, while smaller classes provide a context for expressiveness, nurturance and a more subordinate role for the instructor. In addition, large lecture classes put a physical distance between the professor and her audience, and this in itself increases the likelihood that the students will respond to her on the basis of sex rather than her individual characteristics (15-16).

Discrimination against women professors by women students was reported in Wikler's study as a function of sex-role expectancy, identity problems, and most important, the function of the female professor as a role model/heroine when she is one of a small minority on campus. This attitude may also be a product of the effects of sex-role socialization on female students in leading them to place greater emphasis on the value of having a professor exhibit understanding for the class, make a clear presentation, and be accessible; with their concomitant expectation that women will exhibit these qualities to a greater degree than would men. When women assume the professorial role, and especially when they are teaching larger, more structured undergraduate courses, their demonstration of these qualities may not be in the form expected, desired, and recognized by undergraduate women.

At the same time, male students, who placed a great deal of emphasis on feeling comfortable in class as corollary with teacher effectiveness, may, if they have not resolved their own sexual anxieties, feel particularly uncomfortable with a female authority figure and respond accordingly.

Peterson (1970) suggests that evaluation of a woman's performance by other women is directly proportional to special distinctions awarded that woman and by public recognition. The data from this and other studies show that there is a significant increase in satisfaction between the sophomore and senior years of college. Other significant differences indicated by the study are that math and science professors tend to receive higher ratings from their students than do teachers of other subjects and that older students tend to rate teachers higher than do younger students. These findings support the earlier work of Tolor and others (1973) who suggest that teacher evaluations by students represent a complex interactional process through which all the psychodynamic and social experiences and proclivities of students may be expressed.

The major contribution of our data would seem to be their demonstration of the contradiction students create when they rate women professors significantly higher than their male colleagues on many items of teaching behavior and then rate them significantly lower than men as instructors and rate the courses taught by women professors as having been less good (statistically significantly) than those taught by males. The key to the contradiction may lie in the fact that the items on which females scored significantly higher—enthusiasm, effective course projects, and effective use of audiovisual aids—were neither together nor separately correlated with estimate of instructor and estimate of course, which were the key items.

There are several possibilities for explaining these findings apart from concluding that female professors at Clark University are less effective as teachers than are their masculine colleagues. The problem, however, lies in the circularity of the question itself: If students, consciously or unconsciously, consider their women professors to be less effective teachers, will they, in fact, be taught less effectively by them? If teacher evaluations by students remain a strong criterion measure for determining renewal, tenure, and promotion of women faculty, and students respond on a basis of subjective sex-role stereotyped expectancies, their exposure to women professors is likely to decrease rather than increase with time, and to be reinforced by the continued pattern of low-status women/high-status men.

Our data indicates the following:

1. Students make a distinction based on sex of instructor when they evaluate their professors and courses.

2. A professor's consistency with the sex-role expectations of students plays a strong part in students' evaluations of the former's effectiveness.
3. Sex-role expectancy influences decrease with increased college experience.
4. Placement of women professors as instructors primarily of large, lower-division, undergraduate courses contributes toward making women professors' evaluations lower than those of their male colleagues by virtue of
   a. Women's sex-role socialization behaviors being perceived as more appropriate in a small seminar
   b. Advanced and graduate students demonstrating significantly more positive attitudes toward their professors in evaluating them for reasons that have to do with the circumstances of instruction and status of the students

Conclusions

Sex differences and sex-role expectancies play a major part in evaluating professors of undergraduate courses. Women professors are statistically significantly more harshly evaluated by undergraduate students, male and female. Despite the variety of classroom styles dependent on individual proclivities, students tend to stereotype their professors' behaviors by sex of professor and, to some degree, according to the sex of the student doing the evaluation.

The minority position of women at Clark University contributed to the discrimination against them in student evaluations. There was no opportunity for students — particularly undergraduates — to have had experience of a variety of classroom styles and personal behaviors of women professors that could be anticipated if there had been a large or nearly equal proportion of women to men professors teaching them. This circumstance has enhanced their stereotype of the professor as a male authority figure.

Attribution functions in the socialization process not only by mediating an individual's perceptions of others, but also in resolving conflicts about sex-role identity through pathological behaviors with self-destructive consequences.

Finally, these internalized sex-role criteria are projected in the mediating process in evaluating or resolving cognitive dissonance (i.e., women professors).

Perhaps the ultimate value of these researches is to make more emphatic the need for a non-sex-role-defined world of childhood.

References

Arnold, Magda B. *Motivation and Emotion.* New York: Columbia University Press, 1960. Idem. *Story Sequence Analysis.* New York: Columbia University Press, 1962.

Becker, Howard. *The Outsiders.* "History, Culture and Subjective Experience; An Exploration of the Social Bases of Drug Induced Experiences." In *Youth and Drugs,* edited by McGrath and Scugetti. Glenview, Ill.: Scott Foresman, 1970.

Bernard, Jessie. *Academic Women.* University Park, Pa.: Pennsylvania State University Press, 1964.

Broverman, I.: Vogel, S.; Broverman, D.; Clarkson, F.; Rozenkrantz, P. "Sex Role Stereotypes: A Current Appraisal." *Journal of Social Issues,* no. 2, 1972.

Denmark, Florence, ed. *Who Discriminates Against Women?* Beverly Hills and London: Sage, 1974.

Dissertation Abstracts 29 (1970): 3474.

Farber, Marianne A., and Huber, Joan A., "Sex of Student and Instructor: A Study of Student Bias." *American Journal of Sociology* 80 (1975): 949-63.

Fields, Rona M., and Patrick, Elaine. *The New Feminists. APA Journal* Supplement Abstract Service, July 1975.

Goldberg, Phillip. "Are Women Prejudiced Against Woman?" *Trans-Action,* April 1968, Pp. 28-30.

Kapor-Stanulovic, Nila, and Lynn, David B. "Femininity and Family Planning." *Journal of Sex Research* (1972): 286.

Kelley, Harold H. "Processes of Causal Attribution." In *Current Perspectives in Social Psychology,* edited by Edwin P. Hollander and Raymond G. Hunt. London: University Press, 1976. Pp. 364-74.

Kohlberg L., and Ziegler, W. "The Impact of Cognitive Maturity on the Development of Sex-role Attitudes in the Years 4-8." *Genetic Psychology Monographs,* 1956.

McKee, J. P., and Sheriffs, A.C. "The Differential Evaluation of Males and Females." *Journal of Personality* 25 (1957): 356-71.

Miller, Warren. "A Brief Study on the Psychological Aspects of Unwanted Pregnancy." Paper, 1972.

Newman, Sidney H.; Beck, Mildred B.; and Levits, Sara. *Abortion: Obtained and Denied.* Research approaches published by the Population Council, Bridgeport, Conn., 1971.

Paprocki, E. "Preliminary Personality Test Results; Tehachapi Inmates." Tehachapi California Institution for Men, Research Division, 1960.

Paterson, Gail; Kiesler, Sara, and Goldberg, Phillip. "Evaluation of the Performance of Women as a Function of their Sex, Achievement, and Personal History." *History of Personality and Social Psychology* 19, no. 1 (1971): 114-18.

President's Commission on Law Enforcement, Task Force on Narcotics and Drug Abuse. Washington, D.C.: Government Printing Office, 1969.

Rainwater, Lee. *Family Design.* Chicago: Aldine, 1965. Pp. 185-88.

Scanzoni, John, and McMurray, Martha. "Continuities in the Explanation of Fertility Control." *Journal of Marriage and the Family* 34 (1972): 319.

Sher, Jordan. "Patterns and Profiles of Addiction and Drug Abuse." *Archives of General Psychiatry* 15, November 1966: 539-51.

Strang, Ruth. *Personal Development and Guidance in College and Secondary Schools.* Stanford: Stanford University Press, 1943.

Tolor, A. "Evaluation of Perceived Teacher Effectiveness. *Journal of Educational Psychology* 64 (February 1973): 98.

Wikler, Norma J. "UCSC: Sexism in the Classroom." Unpublished paper, April 1975.

Index